To George Dow
my dad, who modeled the behavior

To Malcolm Gladwell
who gave Connectors a good name

and

To LEADERSHIP Philadelphia Fellows and the Connectors
who connect for the common good

Acknowledgments

This project has been a team effort from the very beginning. We could tell that we were on to something because every time we needed help—from fresh ideas to meeting sites—we got a yes. Everyone involved was generous with their ideas and time. We committed to act in the spirit of Connectors: to share without expecting anything in return. The process has been pure professional joy. We are so grateful for the help of these generous professionals.

The Project Team: John Claypool, Liz Dow, Medard Gabel, Martha Gay, Kate Nelson, Penelope Reed, Chris Satullo, Karen Stephenson, David Thornburgh.

Staff, Focus, and Design Groups: Pauline Abernathy, Mary Stengel Austin, Rob Baron, Barbara Beck, Amanda Bennett, Howard Blumenthal, Renee Booth, Jon Bream, Geneva Campbell, Derrick Carpenter, Richard Clifford, Wade Coleclough, Helen Cunningham, Bernie Dagenais, George Dow, Brian Duke, Dwight Evans, Tom Gailey, Sharon Gallagher, Maureen Garrity, Phil Goldsmith, Victoria Green, Melissa Grimm, David Gull, Julie Hawkins, Dave Hering, Jon Herrmann, Stacy Holland, Colleen Hoy, Catherine Ryan Hyde, Carla Ingram, Sue Jacobson, Farah Jimenez, Alain Joinville, Val Jones, Erik Knudsen, Steve Kurz, Charisse Lillie, Brian Long, James Lynes, Brett Mandel, Bill Marazzo, John McClung, Roz McPherson, Geoffrey Dow McQuilkin, Scottie McQuilkin, Elaine Mercier, Dean Michelson, Bonnie Mueller, Katherine Myers, Kemal Nance, Phyllis Nellis, Jeanne O'Connor, Robert Padullo, Bret Perkins, Ruth Perry, Michelle Porterfield, Dan Rhoton, Doug Richardson, Jenny Rickard, Becky Sanderson, Walt Sarkees, Ellen Savitz, David Seltzer, Alan Sharavsky, Sandy Shea, Laura Shubilla, Tim Stafford, Zack Stalberg, David St. Clair, Suzanne Tavani, Ed Tettemer, Angela Tillar, Kim Turner, Jim Walker, Mailee Walker, Cooper Wardell, Wendy Warren, Melissa Weiler-Gerber, Bob Yermish.

LEADERSHIP Philadelphia's Board of Directors: Craig Adams, Kimberly Allen, Joseph Aristone, Elva Bankins, Elaine Berger, Renee Booth, Tim Boyle, Bob Brown, Patricia Coulter, John DiNome, Nancy Dunleavy, Vernon Francis, Dave Frankel, Joseph Frick, Dan Gallagher, Curtis Gregory, Julie Hawkins, Eileen Heisman, Jennifer Heller, Karen Lessin, Marcus Lingenfelter, Scott Miller, Thomas Nason, Natalye Paquin, Albert Parker, Cherelle Parker, Marsha Perelman, Bret Perkins, Doug Richardson, Jenny Rickard, Woody Rosenbach, Richard Ross, Alexandra Samuels, Jeffrey Scott, Don Smolenski, Diane E. Sullivan, Ed Tettemer, David Thornburgh, Kimberly Turner, Bob Yermish, Michael Zilberfarb.

Connector Subjects (2006 & 2008): see Appendix B

What is
"Six Degrees of Connection"?

Think of that trusted, all-knowing executive assistant. Or the go-to Mom who hears everything first. Or the dry-cleaner who has a finger on the pulse of the neighborhood. You know who I mean: the kind of person who talks to everyone, remembers everything, and acts like a matchmaker without being asked.

Malcolm Gladwell singled them out in *The Tipping Point* as "Connectors": the people who move ideas through society by bridging different worlds. They are the glue that binds corporate cultures, communities, and families. Unlike pay-to-play politicians who make headlines, these leaders often operate under the radar. They are more interested in getting results than getting credit.

Think: George Bailey in *It's a Wonderful Life*. Think: Ben Franklin. Think: Six Degrees of Separation.

Whether you recognize this concept from the Kevin Bacon parlor game or the Will Smith movie, it's a catchy title. But it's really about connection: *Six Degrees of Connection.*

In today's impersonal, BlackBerry-distracted world, with its growing sense of isolation, true connecting is more critical than ever. Connecting is teachable—it's part skill, part attitude, part practice. We've studied these trusted go-to leaders extensively to identify how they operate so that we can teach you the Connectors' way of leading for the long run.

Contents

Part I

Background

"Only Connect"

E.M. Forster

Journey from beach read to your bookshelf

I teach leadership. In the summer of 2000, when I strolled into a bookstore to find a good "beach read," I came upon a book called *The Tipping Point* by Malcolm Gladwell. Drawn to its subtitle, *How Little Things Can Make a Big Difference,* and its length–short enough for a quick read–I picked it up. Perched on the beach and poised to learn, I couldn't put it down. Reading it changed my definition of leadership and a life well lived.

Like the other readers who have kept this book on *The New York Times* Best Seller List for over eight years, I was intrigued by Gladwell's explanation of the way spread through society like epidemics. What really got my attention was his description of the Law of the Few, in which he explained the role of "Connectors" in spreading information and bringing the world together. Suddenly, I had a name for the kind of leadership that inspires me. When Lakers' coach Phil Jackson spoke of pulling together the right players and then getting out of their way, he was acting as a "Connector." When another of my favorite leaders–the late Olympic Hockey coach Herb Brooks–assembled the gold medal winning team, saying, "I'm not looking for the *best* players, I'm looking for the *right* players," he was acting as a "Connector." Even Seabiscuit, famous for his success winning horse races as the underdog, connected a nation during the Depression.

Gladwell's insights helped me to understand why so many of the key leaders who spoke to LEADERSHIP Philadelphia's classes of executives were effective but not inspiring, while certain less traditional and more entrepreneurial leaders mobilized these executives to volunteer to serve the community. These mobilizing leaders are "Connectors." They achieved results by enrolling a diverse group of others in their cause. They earned reputations for serving the common good; they articulated visions that inspired others. Most refreshing of all, they often achieved results by staying under the radar, working behind the scenes with no concern for who received credit.

Gladwell's views struck a chord in so many of us, because not only do we admire these unsung heroes as Connectors, but often we *are* these unsung heroes. Connectors are the kind of everyday hero whom we all know and whom we all can be. Suddenly terms like meritocracy, hometown heroes, and people like George Bailey from the movie *It's A Wonderful Life* come to mind and get the recognition they have earned. Gladwell's "Connectors" are the leaders next door, people like us. Like so many other *The Tipping Point* readers, seeing the possibilities in connection, I wanted to be a better person. Likewise, I wanted to see better people in leadership roles, meaning more "Connectors" who achieve results without caring who gets credit, and who bring out the best in others.

I found myself obsessing over E.M. Forster's comment, "Only connect." The word "connect" seemed to jump out at me everywhere, from "connected" on my computer screen to the "Connect" sign on the City's transport vans. Like other Connectors, I started conversations about *The Tipping Point* with friends and anyone else who would listen. I assigned the book to the participants of LEADERSHIP Philadelphia.

A friend mentioned my near obsession to the local head of Microsoft, who in 2002 brought Gladwell to Philadelphia to speak to employees and community leaders. I was seated across from Gladwell at lunch and had a delightful conversation about his then next book, *Blink*. When he mentioned something about the correlation between salary and height, I told him about a study that quantified that relationship. He had not seen this, so after lunch I sent a broadcast e-mail to my friends who are experts in executive compensation, to find this study. I made sure that the study was in Gladwell's inbox by the time he got home, and it ended up being mentioned in *Blink*.

Coincidentally, *The Philadelphia Inquirer* had been running a series of editorials about City Hall's "Pay to Play" scandals and the lack of local leadership. I approached the Editorial page editor Chris Satullo with the response that Philadelphia has outstanding leadership if you broaden the definition to include Connectors. Chris agreed enthusiastically. This exchange confirmed that we were on the right track.

I was thrilled in 2005 when Gladwell accepted our invitation to speak at a LEADERSHIP Philadelphia alumni event on the Philadelphia stop of his *Blink* book tour. As I prepared his introduction, it dawned on me that the audience was composed of people from various levels of many professional sectors. CEOs would be there sitting next to artists, politicians, doctors, and students. The room seemed to have two of everything—a Noah's Ark of talent. LEADERSHIP Philadelphia is the organizational equivalent of a Connector.

As Gladwell prepared to leave after the speech, I asked him to sign my copy of *Blink.* He inscribed it,

"*To Liz! Philadelphia's #1 Connector.*"

Malcolm Gladwell

The message struck me like a bolt of lightning. It was that day, February 3, 2005, that I decided to focus on the leadership of Connectors. In four years LEADERSHIP, the model for 400 community leadership programs across the country, would be celebrating its 50th anniversary. Instead of simply having another gala event, we would celebrate Connectors. We would change the conversation on leadership in Philadelphia from its focus on what's wrong with local leadership to what's *right*, by broadening the definition of leadership to include "Connectors." We would get that concept into the local language around leadership by identifying Connectors and recognizing their contribution.

When I proposed this idea to my board, they asked about measurable outcomes. What concrete benefit would come out of this work? I told them about an observation that haunted me in Gladwell's *New Yorker* article, "Six Degrees of Lois Weisberg."[1] "If the world is really held together by people like Lois Weisberg . . . how poor you are can be defined quite simply as how far you have to go to get to her . . .

"Poverty is not deprivation.
It is isolation."[2]

The board agreed that we should identify and study Connectors, find out how they operate, and use what we learn to teach kids to connect. If poverty is less about deprivation and more about isolation, let's teach kids to connect their way out of poverty.

Once LEADERSHIP's Board accepted the idea, I called Gladwell to tell him we wanted to identify and study Philadelphia's Connectors. He though that was a good idea. I asked if anyone had ever mapped the Connectors in a city. He chuckled, "No, but *you* could do that!" I replied, "But I don't even know where to start!"

He proceeded to connect me with then Harvard professor and social network guru Karen Stephenson, whom he had interviewed when writing *The Tipping Point.* I e-mailed her and received a call back immediately from Spain. Intrigued by the adventure and creativity of this new application of social network analysis, she was on board immediately.

The Philadelphia Connector Project

Despite its ranking as the fifth largest city in the nation, Philadelphia often acts like a small town. It has the standard cadre of "usual suspects" who tend to run things, win awards for running things, and appear on lists like *Philadelphia Magazine's* "50 Most Powerful People." Given LEADERSHIP's long history and standing in the community and the desire not to discount traditional leaders while discovering new ones, the board debated the pros and cons of taking this non-traditional stand.

This project not only fell into the gray area of innovation, but also had to be handled very carefully from a public relations standpoint. If we were going to try to change the local culture and shine the spotlight away from traditional power players and toward different sorts of people, we needed to be very careful, creative, and clear. We would need the benefit of different types of thinkers who could take a fresh look at leadership in bold new ways.

In true Connector fashion, we assembled a diverse group of professionals with different backgrounds and ways of thinking. The core group—Karen Stephenson, futurist Medard Gabel, ethics professor Kate Nelson, and I—worked this through from the beginning. Each member donated time, expertise, and support wholeheartedly, meeting regularly for three years. We were joined by researcher Martha Gay; architect and planner John Claypool; theatre creative director Penelope Reed; columnist Chris Satullo; and economist David Thornburgh for meeting after meeting. Many others whose names are listed in the Acknowledgments played key roles in the creation and roll-out of the project. This group tailored Stephenson's social network methodology questions to meet our goal of finding community Connectors.

To test the market and to allay the Board's concern about diplomacy and preserving our good relationships, we held six focus groups of local leaders to share our desire and intention to identify, recognize, and research "Connectors" and to praise their style of leadership. The presentation defined Connectors, made the case for Connectors as the new leaders, and included Karen Stephenson's compelling social network analysis. The enthusiastic response created a buzz among local professionals.

We invited the local newspaper editors to the presentation and asked them to assist us in identifying Connectors. They agreed and covered the story as editorials and a feature story.

After laying extensive groundwork and creating the project infrastructure, in the spring of 2006, we solicited nominations, asking the public to identify Connectors.

In Appendix A, I describe the social network analysis done to identify the Connectors. Briefly, we sent a viral e-mail to LEADERSHIP's 2,500 alumni asking them to nominate people and to forward the nomination. The nomination process consisted of providing specific names in response to seven questions around trust. The newspapers wrote stories on the project, referring readers to LEADERSHIP's web site and providing hard copy print nomination forms.

Over 4,800 people submitted 4,300 names in response to the questions. The 101 most frequently listed names were used as the subject of research to determine how Connectors connect.

The research was repeated in 2008 to identify the next generation of Connectors. We were pleased to see that the competencies held true for both experienced and emerging Connectors. The chapters which follow describe Connector competencies and characteristics that differentiate their performance. Competencies are the abilities people bring to a job or situation. They can be developed. They consist of skills and knowledge, which are the outward manifestation of social roles, self-image, traits, and motives.

This book is a handbook that explains what Connectors do and how you can become a Connector—or simply a *better* Connector.

What is a Connector?

Malcolm Gladwell introduced this term into professional mainstream jargon in his perennial best-seller, *The Tipping Point*. According to Gladwell, Connectors link us up with the world, introduce us to our social circles, and possess a special gift for bringing the world together.[3] Connectors are the kind of people who know everyone. They have a gift for making friends and acquaintances. They can be found in any walk of life.

> Gladwell describes Connector Roger Horchow, founder of the high-end mail order Horchow Collection, as "someone with an instinctive and natural gift for making social connections. . . . He's more an observer with the dry, knowing manner of someone who likes to remain a little bit on the outside. He simply likes people, in a genuine and powerful way, and he finds the patterns of acquaintanceship in which people arrange themselves to be endlessly fascinating. Horchow collects people the same way others collect stamps."[4]

Horchow describes Connectors in his book *The Art of Friendship* as people who cultivate acquaintances and friendship for the simple joy of doing so. He believes that a meaningful connection does not necessarily have to imply a lifelong devoted friendship, and that anyone can be a Connector if they take action, make friendships a priority, and understand the importance of following up with people.[5]

Gladwell writes of Chicago Culture Commissioner Lois Weisberg as the prototypical Connector.

> When we talk about power this is usually what we're talking about: money and authority. But there is a third kind of power as well–the kind Lois has–which is a little less straightforward. It's social power.[6]

It's not what you know; it's who you know

Connectors hold a great deal of social capital which, according to Gladwell,

> refers to the resources available in and through personal and business networks. These resources include information, ideas, leads, business opportunities, financial capital, power and influence, emotional support, even goodwill, trust, and cooperation. If you think of human capital as what you know (the sum of your own knowledge, skills, and experience), then access to social capital depends on who you know—the size, quantity, and diversity of your personal and business networks. 'Capital' emphasizes that social capital, like human capital or financial capital, is productive; it enables us to create value, get things done, achieve our goals, fulfill our missions in life, and make our contributions to the world.[7]

It's not about the money

In *The Influentials*, the authors say that affluence is not influence. The book's cover comments state that "For decades these researchers have been on a quest for marketing's holy grail: that elusive but supremely powerful channel known as word of mouth. What they have learned is that even more important than the word–what is said–is the mouth–who says it."[8] Connectors help to drive word of mouth.

It's not about technology

Gladwell expresses concern about the age of isolation and impersonalization driven by the use of computers. He sees that, "paradoxically, all of the sophistication and wizardry and unlimited access to information of the New Economy is going to lead us to rely more on very primitive kinds of social contacts,"[9] like the Connectors. He goes on to say, "When people are overwhelmed with information and develop immunity to traditional forms of communication they turn instead for advice and information to the people in their lives whom they respect, admire and trust."[10] The impact of Facebook, LinkedIn, and sites like Second Life are not yet clear. Gladwell sees Connectors as one cure for the growing sense of isolation and immunity.

Gladwell ends the Afterword of *The Tipping Point* with this message: "In a world dominated by isolation and immunity, understanding these principles of word of mouth is more important than ever." He states that he is "quite sure that there are readers who will use *The Tipping Point* as the inspiration to come up with a way [to use those principles]."[11]

The Philadelphia Connector Project team members were among those readers inspired to do the work to study Connectors to learn more about how to connect. In that way, this book picks up where *The Tipping Point* left off.

Why Connectors Matter

Gladwell writes of Connectors as one antidote to isolation. Social capital experts write of the value that Connectors possess as the tools to make contributions to the world.

In studying Lois Weisberg, Gladwell observed a person who acts as the glue that holds society together. At work, Connectors are the people who foster innovation by bringing together a range of thoughts and thinkers. They work across functional lines to create a culture of collaboration. They hold the institutional memories in a merger. They know how to get things done on a tight deadline.

On the home front, Connectors are the glue that binds the family together. In tough times they can be counted on to listen without judgment and then call on their vast network of acquaintances to solve the problem. When things are going well, they are assembling volunteers, getting the word out about who needs what, and modeling good citizenship for their kids. Using the same respect, listening, and resourcefulness at home as they do outside the home, they raise confident, capable future Connectors.

Connectors matter because they get things done in the community. When we studied Philadelphia's Connectors we were surprised at the number of major projects they helped to accomplish. Among them:

- Created several special schools
- Led foster care reform
- Led City Wage Tax reform movement
- Financed high tech camping, creating over 1000 jobs
- Built the Convention Center, Kimmel Center and National Constitution Center
- Built the sports stadiums
- Created Avenue of the Arts
- Built the world's largest outdoor Mural Program
- Led ethics reform in City government
- Brought the 2000 Republican Convention to the City
- Hosted a LIVE 8 concert, and
- Brought the City back from the brink of financial disaster.

Leadership Louisville is currently replicating our process, which will undoubtedly reveal similar Connector impact: Connectors play a significant role in vitalizing cities.

Malcolm Gladwell says that the world is held together by Connectors like Lois Weisberg, renowned for contributing to the success of countless arts, entrepreneurial, educational, and government endeavors in Chicago. I made a pilgrimage to her office in 2005. Having requested just 20 minutes of her time to learn her thoughts about whether people could be taught to connect, I left nearly two hours later when her assistant pried her away for a lunch obligation.

She was welcoming, attentive, brimming with knowledge, eager to help, and curious about my work. She left me inspired and energized, as Connectors do. She gave me a book on how to change the world, and when I sheepishly asked her to sign my copy of *The New Yorker* article about her, she wrote, "To Liz—you are another one of us."

As I crossed the street from her office to magnificent Millennium Park, just one of Lois's many legacy projects, I vowed to do whatever it took to learn what makes people like Lois tick. My legacy project is to declare that Connectors are the new leaders.

Connectors as a Constant

Benjamin Franklin and Oprah Winfrey are great Connectors. They demonstrate the competencies as follows.

Ben Franklin (1706-1790)

Philadelphia's favorite son, Ben Franklin, founded "Junto," the model for LEADERSHIP Philadelphia, in 1727. As Walter Isaacson noted in his biography of Franklin,[12] Franklin was the consummate networker who "liked to mix his civic life with his social one, and he merrily leveraged both." This statesman, inventor, and entrepreneur demonstrated all of the Connector competencies.

"He that drinks his cider alone,
let him catch his horse alone."

Poor Richard's Almanac[13]

C OMMUNITY CATALYST: Franklin created the Junto for civic and self-improvement. This organization launched a number of civic institutions. "His vision of how to build a new type of nation was both revolutionary and profound."[14]

O THER-ORIENTED: "Franklin's organizational fervor and galvanizing personality made him the most influential force in instilling this as an enduring part of American life."[15]

N ETWORK HUB: The consummate networker, Franklin organized clubs for mutual benefit. He "epitomized this Rotarian urge and has remained, after two centuries, a symbol of it."[16]

N AVIGATING MAZES: Franklin was equally at home among tradesmen, artisans, scientists, and government officials.

E MPOWERING PASSION: Franklin's practice of empowering others: "Would you win the hearts of others, you must not seem to vie with them, but to admire them. Give them every opportunity of displaying their own qualifications."[17]

C URIOUS: Franklin created the American Philosophical Society to promote the sharing of useful knowledge on a wide range of subjects.

T RUSTWORTHY: Franklin "trusted the hearts and minds of his fellow leather-aprons more than he did that of any inbred elite. . . . His trustworthy ways helped to form the nation."[18]

O PTIMISTIC: His guiding principle was a "dislike of everything that tended to debase the spirit of the common people."[19]

R ESULTS ACHIEVER: Junto launched organizations ranging from a lending library to the fire brigades to a hospital to the University of Pennsylvania.

S ELF-STARTER: Franklin created many institutions and worked his way from printer's apprentice to the most famous American of his time.

Oprah Winfrey (b.1954)

Born in rural Mississippi, at 19 Winfrey became a part-time radio reporter in Nashville, and enrolled at Tennessee State University. She dropped out in 1972 to become an anchor at a Nashville television station. She was the first black woman to hold that position.

In 1984, Winfrey accepted a job hosting a Chicago morning talk show, one that aired at the same time as the nationally top-rated, Chicago-based Phil Donahue talk show. With the purchase of a large downtown production facility, Winfrey was able to become the third woman in the American entertainment industry—after Mary Pickford and Lucille Ball—to own her own studio. She named it Harpo, "Oprah" spelled backwards.

Winfrey parlayed her show into a multi-million-dollar business and became the wealthiest black woman in the U.S. In addition to her daytime talk show, she has a successful book club, magazine *O,* the Oprah Winfrey Leadership Academy (a school for girls in South Africa), and has produced Broadway shows and movies. Winfrey launched an XM radio station, "Oprah & Friends," and is launching a channel on the Discovery network. She has become the most powerful and influential woman in television and, according to *Forbes Magazine,* the world's most highly paid entertainer. She is America's consummate Connector!

C **OMMUNITY CATALYST**: Instead of simply being a talk show host, Oprah uses her show as a platform for the common good. She created the Angel Network to help people in need. Her book club launched countless bestsellers and inspires more people to read. Her Leadership Academy in South Africa is growing a generation of women leaders in Africa.

O **THER-ORIENTED**: Oprah's interview style allows well known people to open up in front of an audience of millions. She listens more than she talks during interviews.

N **ETWORK HUB**: *Oprah & Friends XM Radio Show* focuses on a range of subjects and speakers. She offers webinars on important issues.

N **AVIGATES MAZES**: Oprah is not only a leader in the entertainment industry, she also runs and launches businesses, leads a non-profit school, and has actively endorsed a presidential candidate. She relates well to people of all ages and backgrounds.

E **MPOWERING PASSION:** Her enthusiasm, positive attitude, down-to-earth persona, and willingness to disclose vulnerability through her own compelling personal story mobilize others to do more than they thought possible.

C **URIOUS**: Oprah's love of reading reveals her desire to learn, as does her interview style and broad choice of topics to explore.

T **RUSTWORTHY**: Oprah has long-standing friendships and projects an image that she is someone you can talk to and be understood by, but who will not judge you.

O **PTIMISTIC**: She showed fearlessness in starting her first talk show, expanding her empire, and successfully defending a lawsuit brought by Texas cattlemen. She's teaching optimism to the students in the Leadership Academy. She demonstrates resiliency and showcases tales of triumph over adversity.

R ESULTS ACHIEVER: She's earned a fortune by leading an award-winning entertainment enterprise. She has caused millions of book sales, is educating a generation of African girls, and has contributed to the long-term viability of many charities.

S ELF-STARTER: She initiated the Leadership Academy in South Africa. She created a production company and the world's largest webinar. Her bold initiatives are an inspiration to millions of people.

Part II

Connector Competencies

Community Catalyst

"Alexis de Tocqueville pointed out 'the ability of Americans to see the connection between their self-interests and the interests of the community.'"

Jonathan Berry and Ed Keller[20]

Judy Wicks
Founder, White Dog Café

The White Dog Café has been an institution on Philadelphia's University of Pennsylvania campus for over 26 years. A pioneer in the "buy local" food movement, Judy Wicks has built and sustained a reputation for social responsibility and community building.

Judy's entrepreneurial spirit showed up early on in her career when she founded the Free People's Store, now well known as Urban Outfitters, with then husband Dick Hayne in 1970. In the early days, the store served as a community gathering place for West Philadelphia residents, reminiscent of the old-fashioned general store. Recognizing the need for greater community organizing, the couple published the Whole City Catalog, which profiled community organizations in such areas as peace and justice, ecology, social services, and food co-ops.

Judy started the White Dog in 1983 as a take-out muffin shop on the first floor of her house, and she ultimately nurtured it to become a 200-seat restaurant and neighboring retail shop, Black Cat, which sold local and fair trade gifts for over 20 years. The White Dog was sold in 2009 through a unique agreement that preserves the values of the business, such as buying from local farmers, and maintains local independent ownership.

Under Judy's leadership, the White Dog was a place for student camaraderie, family celebrations, and conversations about social justice. The restaurant became a hub for students, faculty, neighbors, and Philadelphia professionals drawn to Judy's vision, great food, and the promise of compelling conversation. Programs included a Table Talk speaker series on issues of public concern, Storytelling Nights for sharing life experiences, a film series, Community Tours of affordable housing, wall murals, prisons, farms and community gardens, and even an international program which took customers and staff on trips to build people-to-people connections in countries such as Nicaragua, Cuba, Vietnam, and the Soviet Union.

When asked when she realized she was a connector, she speaks of her mission. "I am all about supporting the local economy. We buy our produce from local farms, where we can get the best goat cheese, the sweetest strawberries, and the tastiest fresh greens. We've built relationships over the years and count on each other to thrive. Those relationships have given us a competitive advantage in the marketplace. But eventually I realized that if my goal is to support the local economy (not just to maximize our profits), I should share my local food connections with our competitors."

Connectors are community catalysts. Regardless of their formal job description or "day job," they see serving the community as their responsibility. They do an outstanding job of performing their formal duties and layer in a level of community service over and above that.

Community Catalysts have a visionary mindset: the ability to conceptualize greater possibilities and stay focused on the big picture.

Connectors relate their own work and what is happening in the community to specific needs of others. They see patterns and long-term consequences of short-term actions. They understand and assess risk well. They relate the implication of their own work and what is happening in the community to specific needs of others.

Connectors are energized by collaborating with others to solve unusual, complex, or large-scale problems. While keeping their eye on the big picture, they pay attention to detail and mobilize resources to complete tasks. They help others to understand the larger business and community context in order to identify possibilities for the future.

Connectors "think big" by seeing the potential for what could be accomplished if the right resources were aligned. They challenge colleagues and acquaintances at work and at home to rethink business strategies and approaches in order to be competitive for the long-term.

SELF ASSESSMENT

Instructions: Please rate yourself on the following behaviors. A (1) means that this is never true of you, while a (5) means that you always do this.

EXERCISE
Are you a Community Catalyst?

1. I think about the impact of my work on the community.

1	2	3	4	5
never	rarely	sometimes	usually	always

2. I let colleagues know about civic initiatives that may affect them.

1	2	3	4	5
never	rarely	sometimes	usually	always

3. I am energized by collaborating with others on large projects with significant impact.

1	2	3	4	5
never	rarely	sometimes	usually	always

4. I think big but also make sure that details are handled.

1	2	3	4	5
never	rarely	sometimes	usually	always

5. I think and talk about my city/town/neighborhood's strengths and potential.

1	2	3	4	5
never	rarely	sometimes	usually	always

6. I challenge others to take responsibility for the future of this region.

1	2	3	4	5
never	rarely	sometimes	usually	always

7. I step back to look at how the parts of the project fit together to achieve the entire goal.

1	2	3	4	5
never	rarely	sometimes	usually	always

8. When planning I create different scenarios, taking public and private sector implications into consideration.

1	2	3	4	5
never	rarely	sometimes	usually	always

9. I cultivate ties in the public, private and non-profit sectors.

1	2	3	4	5
never	rarely	sometimes	usually	always

10. I identify with my city and feel an obligation to give back.

1	2	3	4	5
never	rarely	sometimes	usually	always

11. I intend to leave my legacy in the city where I live now.

1	2	3	4	5
never	rarely	sometimes	usually	always

12. I see aspects of my work as a calling.

1	2	3	4	5
never	rarely	sometimes	usually	always

13. I put myself in a position to understand and affect local issues and perspectives.

1	2	3	4	5
never	rarely	sometimes	usually	always

14. I choose to take on more in my job than others do in a similar job.

1	2	3	4	5
never	rarely	sometimes	usually	always

15. I am capable of articulating a vision that inspires others to act.

1	2	3	4	5
never	rarely	sometimes	usually	always

Identify (circle) one behavior to improve in the next year.

Lessons learned from Connectors on being a Community Catalyst

1. Connectors are able to convey a vision that moves and engages others. They paint a verbal picture that others find compelling and therefore, want to support. Others sense that what the Connector sees can happen, and they want to help make it happen.

2. Connectors have at their fingertips a network of peers who trust the quality of their work and know that he or she is reliable. When the Connector comes up with a big idea, he/she tests it on members of the network who are eager to engage and to be supportive.

3. Connectors tend to focus on the future and develop and share alternative scenarios. They enjoy being informed of creative endeavors, and they assemble people to find new ways to solve problems.

4. Connectors have a global perspective. They read about current affairs and are aware of what is going on around the world. They see themselves as a national or global citizen, above and beyond their local community identity.

5. Connectors seek meaning and are driven to make a difference. This drive carries over into their work, which they then see as a calling rather than as a job. They are energized by the portion of their work that allows them to feel that they are serving others.

6. Connectors have a servant leader mentality. They value the opportunity to serve others, and also see service as one's obligation as a citizen. They treat others as attentively as good businesses treat customers. They respect the humanity in others.

7. Connectors see opportunities to serve all around them. They are attuned to the need to help others, and are willing to roll up their sleeves and pitch in. They believe that their contribution will be valuable and welcome.

8. Connectors behave as though they always have excess capacity available to serve a good cause. They rarely refuse to help because they are too busy. They will take on added civic responsibility because they feel honored and obliged to serve the greater good.

9. Connectors win others over with contagious energy and well crafted images. They invite a broad range of people to share in their dreams. Their track record and reputation give others the confidence that time and energy invested with Connectors is worthwhile.

10. Connectors take off their blinders. They are not constrained by the desire to work and collaborate with like-minded people who look and think as they do. They are eager to form diverse coalitions of others who want to be part of something bigger than themselves. They find those alliances uplifting.

Behaviors that derail the ability to be Community Catalysts

1. Focusing on the details to such an extent that you miss the big picture. Laboring over small tasks so intently that you fail to step back to ask yourself what purpose this effort serves.

2. Failure to incorporate the contributions of other functions or parts of the organization or community into decisions because you are in too much of a hurry or because you do not see the value of input from other disciplines and viewpoints. This can lead to simplistic solutions.

3. Developing a reputation for only caring about your own cause. Consistently placing self-interest over that of the greater good: not behaving as a team player.

4. Measuring the return on investment so narrowly that you fail to see larger opportunities to leverage your service or product: thinking small.

5. Putting your ambition and need for recognition and reward above the work. Doing only what is necessary to achieve your immediate short-term goal.

6. Being overly focused on developing and using your technical skills at the expense of developing the ability to work and share ideas with others. Letting your professional pride prevent you from collaborating with people from other disciplines or who are "too junior."

7. Micromanaging your team so that they are neither encouraged to think outside the box nor rewarded for doing so. Discouraging brainstorming and creative approaches to problem-solving.

8. Lacking the passion and conviction required to engage others in your vision. Keeping your creative dreams to yourself because you fear that they will not be appreciated or that others will steal or misuse them.

9. Putting in the minimum amount of effort required to come up with a solution. Going with the obvious solution because it is easy and you see no point in doing more than anyone else. Looking left and right to make sure that you're not working any harder than you have to. Conceiving of your assignment as "just work" rather than something to be proud of.

10. Ignoring the challenges and opportunities faced by your city. Assuming that the city survives through inertia and bureaucracy and that nothing that you do matters or helps or hurts the city. Criticizing government workers and civil servants and underestimating their value and contribution.

Ten ways to become a Community Catalyst

At work

1. Find out what your organization does to support the community. What charities does it support? How are charitable contribution decisions made? On which non-profit boards do executives serve? Which boards would your organization like you to serve on? How does your business define its obligation to the community?

2. Introduce yourself to someone who works in your organization's government relations function. Find out what your company does in that area. Become familiar with corporate priorities in relation to the public sector. Are there important regulatory constraints or opportunities to share information?

3. Read your local paper and local business and trade journals. Familiarize yourself with local trends and priorities. Watch for business opportunities as well as other areas in which you could make a difference.

4. Reinforce big picture thinking. Reward people who do community service or cultivate contacts outside of the office. Build a reputation for reaching out beyond the walls of your company.

At home

5. Instead of focusing on what you want your children to be like now, think about the kind of person you want them to be at age 40. Listen attentively for their specific gifts and interests. Watch for the clues as to the oak within the acorn. Write out your vision for them and think through what it will take to get them there. Work backwards from the vision and write down what you can do in the next year to support their development and their dreams. This can range from adding to your college savings plan to convincing them to read the newspaper or to take a class in acting. Think big on behalf of your kids.

6. Encourage and support any activities that broaden your child's perspective. Let them know that the world outside of your neighborhood is inviting, fascinating, safe, and full of opportunity. Broaden their perspective.

7. Encourage your children to participate in team sports and team activities. Involve them in efforts that include people from different backgrounds and cultures. Encourage your children to spend time with their grandparents and elders. Talk about the positive side of aging.

8. Introduce yourself and your family to the people who make the community work. Talk to the postman about how mail gets delivered. Stop at the police and fire station with your children to introduce them to these first responders and ask them about their work. Teach your children not to take their community for granted.

In the community

9. Get involved in township or other local community efforts. Choose an issue that matters to you and find out how to take a leadership position.

10. Invite a local politician to your home or place of worship to give him/her an opportunity to get to know your neighbors. Raise issues about what is going well, and ask how you and your neighbors can volunteer to serve the community.

"Community Garden. It's not just about the vegetables."

Sign at the College of St. Catherine,
St. Paul, Minnesota

Other-Oriented

*"Seek first to understand,
then to be understood."*

Stephen R. Covey[21]

SOZI TULANTE
Partner, Hangley, Aronchick, Segal & Pudlin

Originally from Zaire (now the Democratic Republic of Congo), Sozi Tulante immigrated to North Philadelphia in 1983 after the United States granted his family asylum and following his father's release as a political prisoner. Far from the magical land he had imagined, America was at first gritty, unfamiliar, and uninviting to Sozi and his family. They were desperately poor and utterly isolated. Sozi probably developed his Connector skills around this time as a means to survive. He discovered how to read non-verbal cues and to fit into any situation so that others—teachers, fellow students, neighbors—could be more at ease with his difference.

Finding refuge in his schoolbooks, Sozi excelled academically and, due to his parents' prodding, was accepted to Harvard. When he completed college, Harvard Law School came calling and after three years, awarded him a degree with honors. In seven years at Harvard, Sozi's Connector skills again served him well as he befriended students and professors of diverse backgrounds, races, and interests.

He has now resettled in Philadelphia and has immersed himself in politics and public service. He serves on the board of the refugee agency that relocated his family two decades ago. He is also a community leader in West Philadelphia, where he makes his home with his wife and their infant son.

Sozi has consciously developed ways to build bridges with others. He does this through his love of soccer, which is not only a sport but a passion shared by billions globally. Because of his knowledge about soccer, he connects with a wide range of friends, neighbors, colleagues, and clients everywhere he travels. Every four years, he attends the World Cup to fuel this passion.

As a trivia buff, Sozi can comfortably banter about just about any topic under the sun, a talent he displayed when appearing on the television show "Jeopardy" in 2002. Using what originated as a means to assimilate into a new culture, the Connector skills demonstrated by Sozi increasingly benefit the Philadelphia community.

Other-Oriented people have the ability to interact and build rapport effectively across a wide range of social situations.

Connectors make others feel comfortable by reading their non-verbal cues accurately and quickly adapting to the other person. They listen intently in such a way that the other person feels heard. They strive to find common ground despite apparent surface level differences. They come across to others as modest.

People who demonstrate this competency have "never met a stranger." They have a wide comfort zone and welcome contact with a broad range of people. This is not to be confused with the stereotype of people who can "sell ice to Eskimos," for such individuals are not likely to display the Connectors' authenticity. They approach others as equals and, while understanding rank, do not dole out respect as if it were a scarce resource.

Connectors actively seek out people who are different from them and take pleasure in understanding others' perspectives. They share information about themselves openly but appropriately as they build rapport.

SELF ASSESSMENT

Instructions: Please rate yourself on the following behaviors. A (1) means that this is never true of you, while a (5) means that you always do this.

EXERCISE
Are you Other-Oriented?

1. I establish rapport with others quickly and easily.

1	2	3	4	5
never	rarely	sometimes	usually	always

2. I know how to put strangers at ease.

1	2	3	4	5
never	rarely	sometimes	usually	always

3. I can move a conversation beyond chit-chat to something of substance.

1	2	3	4	5
never	rarely	sometimes	usually	always

4. I read non-verbal cues well, and adjust my communication accordingly.

1	2	3	4	5
never	rarely	sometimes	usually	always

5. I am comfortable talking with people who are outside of my circle of friends/acquaintances.

1	2	3	4	5
never	rarely	sometimes	usually	always

6. I can find common ground with just about anyone fairly quickly.

1	2	3	4	5
never	rarely	sometimes	usually	always

7. People tell me that I'm easy to talk to, and they open up to me.

1	2	3	4	5
never	rarely	sometimes	usually	always

8. My friends and family tell me I'm a good listener.

1	2	3	4	5
never	rarely	sometimes	usually	always

9. I strive to focus on others and to give them my undivided attention.

1	2	3	4	5
never	rarely	sometimes	usually	always

10. Right after I meet someone, I can describe his or her interests to others.

1	2	3	4	5
never	rarely	sometimes	usually	always

11. I am willing and able to share information about myself in order to connect.

1	2	3	4	5
never	rarely	sometimes	usually	always

12. I believe that every connection I make is worthwhile and may be of value to someone in some way in the future.

1	2	3	4	5
never	rarely	sometimes	usually	always

13. People would describe me as modest and experience me as humble.

1	2	3	4	5
never	rarely	sometimes	usually	always

14. I set my competitive instincts aside when I first meet someone.

1	2	3	4	5
never	rarely	sometimes	usually	always

15. I listen respectfully to viewpoints that differ from mine and try to find points of agreement.

1	2	3	4	5
never	rarely	sometimes	usually	always

Identify (circle) one behavior to improve in the next year.

Lessons learned from Connectors about being Other-Oriented

1. Connectors believe they can learn something from everyone they meet, so they give everyone their full attention. This includes colleagues, family, friends, acquaintances, and people they encounter in routine interactions. Waiters, the check-out person at the supermarket, the person in the elevator with you, the receptionist and crossing guard, all have stories to tell and deserve, at the very least, eye contact and a smile. Connectors make it their goal to cause the other person to feel better as a result of their contact, if only for an instant.

2. While rank is one factor to consider when you communicate with another person, Connectors tend to place less importance on this factor than others. By doing this, Connectors expand the range of people with whom they feel comfortable. This means that they are less intimidated by very high-level people, who they assume are just like the rest of us in most ways. They also see the humanity in others from cultures or worlds that differ from their own, believing that inside they are alike and therefore have things in common. They hold a world view that we are all connected.

3. Connectors are adept at assembling teams with complementary viewpoints and expertise. Rather than surrounding themselves with like-minded people of the same rank or from similar backgrounds, they seek contributors who bring a range of perspectives to the table. Connectors seek solutions that incorporate a variety of ways of thinking.

4. Connectors can demonstrate a bystander mentality. They sit back and take in the views of others. This behavior removes the distraction of worrying about what they will say next and frees them up to hear what others have to say. They focus on the big picture of what is happening in the room or at the table. By doing this, they begin to form what Quakers call "a sense of the meeting." This means that by freeing themselves from focusing on their own thoughts (which they already know), Connectors

enable themselves to take in the mix of contributions in the room, allowing them to reframe the way they see things to incorporate the views of others. They then can repeat to the others points of agreement that need further work, thereby moving groups to consensus.

5. Connectors are tactful and committed to preserving the dignity of others. They find ways to make others feel good about themselves. If another makes a mistake in a meeting, the Connector uses good-natured humor to deflect criticism from that person, or makes a point of saying something kind yet authentic to that person after the meeting. He or she looks for opportunities to make specific compliments, whether it is singling someone out for specific deserved praise in a meeting or making a kind comment about the pin that a sales-woman chose to wear that day. Connectors make that little extra effort to lift another's spirit in significant or small ways, ever aware of others' need to feel valued.

6. Connectors are skilled at group process. They work to establish goals and roles when the group first forms. They make sure that each member of the group is introduced to the others so that everyone is aware of the capabilities present in the room. By clarifying goals, Connectors make sure participants become united around a cause and use their time efficiently. Connectors make sure that each person knows his or her role in order to make sure that there is no redundancy. Connectors understand, respect, and openly acknowledge the value of others' contributions.

7. Connectors reveal vulnerable parts of themselves, when doing so will help others to feel understood. Letting your guard down to allow another person in distress to know that you have made similar mistakes or faced similar challenges and survived is empowering to the other person. Connectors explain what they did wrong and how they corrected the problem, got past their sense of failure or embarrassment, and moved on to wholeness. This helps give the other person a roadmap. While many people believe that revealing weaknesses will cost them the respect of others, Connectors believe that being forthcoming about past

failures opens up channels of communication and lets others know that they are accepted and understood.

8. Connectors make an effort to be useful to others. They listen vigilantly to discover what the other person wants. In this way, they demonstrate a constant customer service orientation, meaning that they see everyone as a customer whom they can serve. At work, they are alert for opportunities to contribute to a project. At home they listen carefully to what their family and friends are excited about, with the intention of helping them get what they need or finding a way to contribute time and effort related to the others' interests. In the community, they look for opportunities to volunteer to help local organizations.

9. Connectors make an effort to make others feel important. This begins with eye contact and a smile, and progresses as the Connector looks for ways—big and small—to make the other person look or feel good. This behavior ranges from making sure to give credit to others who have contributed to an effort, to giving specific praise to them and to others about them. Their small touches include sending notes to acknowledge others' successes or special events, praising the waiter in front of his boss, and telling the receptionist how he/she brightens the Connector's day. In shining the spotlight on others and away from him/herself, the Connector is experienced by others to be modest, humble, and accessible.

10. Connectors work to be fully present when they are with others. They give others their undivided attention. While they may be angry, stressed, or busy, their commitment to make others feel acknowledged overrides their other distractions. They are vigilant about staying engaged in productive conversation and making the current conversation their top priority. This means that they turn off their cell phones and BlackBerrys and set aside preoccupations while they meet with others. This signals to others that the conversation between them is important. In the presence of a Connector, others feel seen, heard, and understood.

Behaviors that derail Other-Orientation

1. Taking calls on your cell phone or BlackBerry, or sending or receiving text messages in the middle of a conversation, meeting, or meal.

2. Ignoring people below your perceived rank or pay grade; only managing up. Assuming that power is based exclusively upon formal titles.

3. Guiding all conversation toward your own needs and goals to ensure that your needs and goals are understood and met, with little concern for the needs of the other person.

4. Looking everywhere other than directly in the other person's eye. In particular, looking at your watch while the other person is talking, or worse still, looking past the person you are talking to in search of someone you deem to be more important or interesting, thereby causing the other to feel dismissed.

5. Assembling a group for a purpose and failing to introduce the team members to each other, thereby missing the opportunity for members to fully understand the resources available within the team.

6. Engaging in conversations aimed at showing the other person that you are right and they are wrong, and/or that you are superior to them in some way, implying that they should accept the fact that they are inferior.

7. Signaling a sense of entitlement that for some reason (which you feel should be obvious to others), you deserve superior treatment or benefits. When this assumption is not shared or acted upon by others, you express your disdain, disgust, or inconvenience.

8. Holding partisan views so strongly that you are unwilling to listen respectfully to people whose views differ from yours. This may manifest itself as dominating a conversation or deriding and

dismissing another person who disagrees, causing the other to disengage or check out of the conversation.

9. Acting on a world view that stresses differences over similarities. This includes stereotyping others and drawing conclusions about other views and behaviors not on their individual merit, but rather based upon your beliefs and perspectives. Concluding that your beliefs are the only right beliefs and those who don't share them are not only wrong but inferior.

10. Climbing the ladder professionally or socially by stepping on others, taking credit for others' successes, and making yourself look good at others' expense. Forgetting where you came from and leaving behind in a cloud of dust those who helped you to succeed. This includes only putting out effort for people who you believe will be useful in meeting your goals.

Ten ways to increase your Other-Orientation

At Work

1. Think of yourself as the host in any meeting you attend. Without formally usurping the role of the actual convener, make the effort to introduce yourself to participants whom you don't know, or to introduce participants to each other. This fundamental courtesy is ignored far too often in meetings, and the others around the table will appreciate your thoughtfulness in making introductions.

2. When you enter someone's office, notice what they have chosen to display or to hang on the walls. Ask questions about items that seem unique or themes that emerge. They have selected these decorations, and each probably has a story behind it, which you should strive to remember. Better still, make an effort to add to their collection.

3. Take responsibility for making colleagues, clients, and customers comfortable in your presence. Make the effort to know about

their interests beyond the immediate transactions at hand. Do not assume that the other person is just passing through your life to complete the tasks you are working on; instead, be open to the possibility that the relationship may become more enduring or multifaceted.

At Home

4. Start playing games like *Life Stories* in which you encourage kids and adults to share stories that broaden each others' horizons and help friends and family members to really get to know each other, beyond basic family folklore and stereotypes.

5. Encourage grandparents or older neighbors to tell your children stories about their youth. Ask them specifics like how they celebrated holidays or what they did in school or on the weekends or about their family rituals. Encourage them to think of small kindnesses to do for one another.

6. Ask the adults who visit your home to tell your kids about their work, and how they decided to do what they do. Ask them where they went to college, why they went there, and what they liked or didn't like about the jobs they have had. Mix people of different generations together and orchestrate conversations of substance.

7. Work on noticing what is unique about your family members and friends, and discuss this in a positive way. Rather than staying at the level of describing sports events, the roads you took to get somewhere, and the weather, talk about what's unique and positive about the people you interact with in and outside of your home. Doing this requires listening and learning to draw others out, but the effort will be repaid in forming stronger connections. Your children are more likely to listen to others if they have been listened to at home.

In the Community

8. Identify one or two people with whom you interact routinely,

such as your dry cleaner, the person who helps you at the post office, the checkout person at the grocery store, or the clerk where you buy your morning coffee. Do you know the names of these people—or anything else about their lives? At least get to know their names and look them in the eye and thank them for their work. If they seem tired or irritated, tell them something positive about their impact on you or their customers. Make it your job to help them to feel valued next time you interact.

9. Does it ever occur to you that you are lucky to have caught a cab, that the driver is taking you where you need to go, or that the driver is a person with a life outside of the cab? Many cab drivers are immigrants who have arrived in your town through an adventure and great effort. Most are very grateful to be in America and to have a job. Next time you step in a cab, ask the driver where they are from and how they chose your city. Thank cabbies, bus drivers, and flight attendants for their service. You'll brighten their day and your own.

10. Drop by your local fire station and tell the firefighters how much you appreciate their work. Bring your kids along if you have any. If a firefighter appears to have the time and interest to talk, ask them what he or she likes like about the job and what lessons they have learned, and listen to what they say. Be sure to say something positive about what you hear before you leave.

"How far you can go in life depends on being tender with the young, compassionate with the aged, sympathetic with the striving, and tolerant of the weak and the strong. Because someday in life you will have been all of these."

George Washington Carver

Network Hub

"They have a network of contacts broader not only than the norm for society but also broader than the networks of people often named as demographically desirable, for example: the affluent."

Jonathan Berry and Ed Keller[22]

CHRIS SATULLO

Executive Director of News and Civic Dialogue,
WHYY Public Radio

During Chris Satullo's long run as the Editorial Page Editor of *The Philadelphia Inquirer,* he defined his job as connecting with people and the ideas that would help them— from global to local, political to spiritual. The journalist's job is to make sense of the connections. He sees the newspaper as an indispensable tool of connection. The role of a network hub is to continuously expand relationships in the community to increase the interconnectedness of networks. Chris does this by telling people to talk to other people who can add a piece to their puzzle, because "people who have a problem often have no clue who else is working on it, so they waste energy reinventing the wheel."

Network building starts with the mindset Chris describes, "I'm interested in almost everything. I'm never bored by any topic. There is no topic I don't want to hear about. Journalists know that if you assume that some people aren't interesting, you'll miss a world of possibilities. No matter what, there's a story in there."

He believes that Connectors shift from official contact to friendly contact and include a variety of people in their social world. Rather than being dismissive of people who are different, Connectors are enthusiastic about meeting them.

Chris describes a defining moment that demonstrates the way network hubs think and work, "In January of 1999, we did the first big Citizen's Voices project on the Mayor's race. I was in a different neighborhood every night running forums–driving to another part of Philadelphia that I had never seen before. I'd get there and meet another 20 people trying to make a difference, sharing policy ideas I never knew. This is a vast place in need of saving. They deserve to be helped, and we should help them. It's a useful thing for a journalist to fall in love with the city they are working for."

Chris took this a step further by forging a partnership between the newspaper and the University of Pennsylvania, called the Penn Project for Civic Engagement. Chris led the Great Expectations project, convening hundreds of citizens to give voice to their priorities and to create an agenda for Philadelphia's future. Chris and fellow Connector Harris Steinberg continued this process in the areas of waterfront development, use of the Kimmel Center public space, and a wide range of civic topics.

This creative convening of citizens has promoted a form of deliberate democracy that unites the city. Their work has received national recognition for its effectiveness. In typically modest fashion, Chris would tell you that the work speaks for itself and that this is not about the people who do it.

Network Hubs continuously expand the breadth and depth of relationships in the community to increase the interconnectedness of networks.

Connectors make a conscious effort to build relationships with individuals throughout the community, even when there is no obvious benefit involved. They proactively ask people questions to better understand their backgrounds, areas of interest and expertise, and their needs. They grow networks by sharing information and expertise.

Connectors take inventory of what they learn from and about others in conversations. They draw upon this inventory in future situations to help connect people to one another as potential resources. They broker relationships even when there is no personal gain. They leverage relationships built on trust to quickly gain access to appropriate parties and deepen understanding of people's needs. These capabilities and connections make them hubs of network activities and the link between unusual numbers and kinds of people. They often invite these people to come together on behalf of the community.

SELF ASSESSMENT

Instructions: Please rate yourself on the following behaviors. A (1) means that this is never true of you, while a (5) means that you always do this.

EXERCISE
Are you a Network Hub?

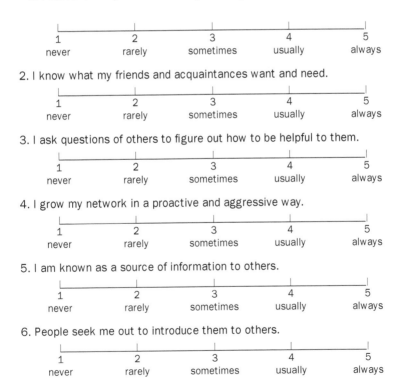

1. I strive for win/win solutions by seeking mutual benefit in my dealings.

1	2	3	4	5
never	rarely	sometimes	usually	always

2. I know what my friends and acquaintances want and need.

1	2	3	4	5
never	rarely	sometimes	usually	always

3. I ask questions of others to figure out how to be helpful to them.

1	2	3	4	5
never	rarely	sometimes	usually	always

4. I grow my network in a proactive and aggressive way.

1	2	3	4	5
never	rarely	sometimes	usually	always

5. I am known as a source of information to others.

1	2	3	4	5
never	rarely	sometimes	usually	always

6. People seek me out to introduce them to others.

1	2	3	4	5
never	rarely	sometimes	usually	always

7. I am confident that when I reach out to someone, I can get a response.

1	2	3	4	5
never	rarely	sometimes	usually	always

8. I am active on local boards and other volunteer activities.

1	2	3	4	5
never	rarely	sometimes	usually	always

9. I seek acquaintances from different organizations, neighborhoods, and backgrounds.

1	2	3	4	5
never	rarely	sometimes	usually	always

10. I suspend judgment about others when I first meet them, to seek points of connection.

1	2	3	4	5
never	rarely	sometimes	usually	always

11. I convene people from different backgrounds to work on volunteer projects.

1	2	3	4	5
never	rarely	sometimes	usually	always

12. I cultivate weak ties by sending emails to check in, and thank you notes and cards.

1	2	3	4	5
never	rarely	sometimes	usually	always

13. I see synergies and similarities between people that others miss.

1	2	3	4	5
never	rarely	sometimes	usually	always

14. I use my connections and social capital to help others.

1	2	3	4	5
never	rarely	sometimes	usually	always

15. I have a broad range of interests and experiences, which I draw upon to build relationships with others.

1	2	3	4	5
never	rarely	sometimes	usually	always

Identify (circle) one behavior to improve in the next year.

Lessons Learned from Connectors about Network Hubs

1. In *The Seven Habits of Highly Successful People,* Stephen Covey writes about the concept of the abundance mentality.[23] Connectors hold this world view, believing that there is plenty out there for everyone. They are therefore willing and eager to contribute to others' success. Their win/win mentality assumes that "one person's success is not achieved at the expense or exclusion of the success of others."[24]

2. Connectors enjoy introducing people to each other for the others' mutual benefit. They then walk away to allow the others to move their new connection forward. Connectors make the introduction because they seek benefit for the others, not because they see benefit for themselves. They demonstrate a "pay it forward" mentality.

3. Connectors, unlike traditional networkers, are seeking help for others when they connect. Traditional networkers tend to be looking for help for themselves. In making this selfless effort, Connectors earn a reputation for generosity that draws others to them and increases the likelihood that others will return their calls.

4. Connectors go out of their way to introduce people to each other at meetings, parties, and events. They are sensitive to the need for newcomers to meet people and go out of their way to make others feel welcome, regardless of who convened the meeting, event, or party.

5. Connectors are not simply conduits that pass information around. Because they have the ability and desire to influence others, Connectors can incite a network to action and mobilize others for a cause.

6. Connectors hold onto contacts over the course of years by making small gestures to stay in touch. Unlike many people, they do not

only contact someone when they need a favor from them. They reach out in proactive ways simply to be positive and kind.

7. Connectors know that everyone has a story, so they make an effort to learn that story. They ask clarifying questions and listen intently to answers. Because Connectors also exhibit trust and discretion, they get others to open up to them to a degree that the other sometimes finds surprising. Others express to Connectors that "I feel like I have known you forever," or "I've told you things that I haven't told my own family." This behavior continues because the Connector keeps the information confidential.

8. Connectors see synergies between people that others miss. It is not uncommon for Connectors to introduce two people who work for the same company or live in the same neighborhood (often not the Connector's company or neighborhood). They take the time to ask people questions. They listen well and remember others' answers. In so doing they build a wealth of knowledge, which they use to bring people together.

9. Connectors tend to have a very broad range of personal interests, and therefore have something to say in a broad range of conversations. They enjoy conversations that move from business to current events to children's accomplishments to good movies and travel. They are facile at switching subjects so they can connect with people on a variety of topics. This enables them to be interested in and interesting to a wide range of people.

10. Connectors seek novelty in people, projects, and information. They embrace new people and ideas with enthusiasm, eager to make sense of new information. They seek the challenge of newness, which seems to satisfy a sort of inner restlessness that keeps them moving ahead. They tend not to get excited by the status quo and are comfortable leading or embracing change.

Behaviors that derail becoming a Network Hub

1. Demonstrating the need to be involved in every match made with others, as opposed to making an introduction and letting those introduced take it from there.

2. Waiting to be asked to lunch, volunteer activities, and other social events instead of reaching out to get involved.

3. Assuming that your social or professional circle is already complete, and that widening it would be too much work with too little reward.

4. Freezing out newcomers to your company, town, or neighborhood, assuming that the outsiders have nothing of value to offer and that welcoming them is either unnecessary or not your responsibility.

5. Sticking exclusively with people who look and act like you and share your values, politics, and demographics. Assuming that you have little in common with those other people, so you miss the opportunity to learn from them and broaden your knowledge.

6. Acting on the assumption that in order for you to win or look good, someone else must lose or look bad. Maneuvering to discredit and disenfranchise others for your own personal gain.

7. Believing that your first impressions about people are always right. Failing to demonstrate patience and take a closer look for areas of similarity and agreement.

8. Convincing yourself that you are shy and introverted and could not possibly speak to strangers or other new people because you would not know what to say. This includes convincing yourself that they would find you uninteresting or otherwise lacking, so that you give up without trying to reach out.

9. Keeping conversations at such a superficial level (weather, sports, traffic, food) that you miss the opportunity to get to know anything

of substance about the other person. Filling conversations with trivia so that when you walk away you know no more about the other person than when you met.

10. Assuming that someone else will take the lead on a cause or that your voice or vote on a community issue does not count. Passively accepting behaviors, decisions, or actions that go against your beliefs about community because you are too busy or disengaged to step up and take action.

Ten Ways to become a Network Hub

At work

1. Attend as many formal and informal gatherings as possible. Make an effort to get to know people throughout the organization at all levels. Welcome new employees and let them know that you are available to answer questions.

2. When assembling project teams, err on the side of inclusion. Map out the stakeholders involved and invite their representatives to be involved when practical.

3. Identify five people in your company whom you find interesting. Invite them to breakfast or lunch and learn more about them. Once you have met those five, find five more and repeat the exercise.

At home

4. Host a block party to introduce neighbors to each other. If this seems daunting, host a small party for 6 people who you would like to meet or who you think would like each other. Learn about your neighbors' work and family interests.

5. Talk about age-appropriate current events with your children at the dinner table. Give each person the opportunity to share something interesting that they learned in order to encourage

them to speak up and to expand their horizons.

6. Post a U.S. or world map on a wall in the house. Teach your children where key events happened. Tell them stories about your travels or about the history of different sites. Place dots on the places that you have been or would like to go. Plan vacations in places that you've never been. Ask the kids to read about the places before you go to teach you (and them) something about it. Find opportunities to share favorable impressions and insights.

In the community

7. Take a leadership role in your place of worship. Assemble people around an operating issue, cause, or educational opportunity. Make sure that meetings include time for introductions and socializing.

8. Assemble neighbors to meet with a local elected official about an issue of mutual concern. Set aside time in the meeting for each person to introduce him/herself and tell the others where he/she works and one of their interests.

9. Next time you go out for drinks or a meal after a game, ask everyone to share their best job and worst job, and keep the conversation focused on learning more about each other.

10. Take your family to visit a house of worship for a faith other than your own. Look up something about that religion beforehand and discuss the ways in which it is like yours. Take the family to lunch afterwards to discuss what you observed.

"*Influentials [like Connectors] are the strategically placed transmitters that amplify the signal, multiplying dramatically the number of people who hear it.*"

Jonathan Berry and Ed Keller[25]

Navigating Mazes

"Somehow she [Lois Weisberg] managed to be plausible as a flea-market peddler to a bunch of flea-market peddlers, the same way she managed to be plausible as a music lover to a musician like Tony Bennett. It doesn't matter who she's with or what she's doing; she always manages to be in the thick of things."

Malcolm Gladwell[26]

DAVID THORNBURGH

Executive Director, The Fels Institute of Government,
The University of Pennsylvania

David Thornburgh grew up in a family deeply engaged in its community. His father, Dick, served as US Attorney in Pittsburgh, was elected Governor of Pennsylvania in 1978, and served as US Attorney General under Presidents Reagan and Bush. David's mother Ginny is a passionate advocate for the rights of people with disabilities. Inspired by his parents' passion for public service, David has the reputation of being someone who works across sectors for the common good.

David possesses a natural curiosity that has inspired his ability to connect. He attributes his effectiveness as a Connector to several core attitudes. He believes that it's important to have a balanced sense of reciprocity. "You have to be willing and comfortable to give before you can receive. You need to make deposits in the favor bank before you can make withdrawals. You have to like people and be energized by their passions. This 'passion to passion' connection is how you establish a bond. Real Connectors are about 'connecting' people, not 'collecting' people. This is not about self-interest. It's about trust."

When David ran the Alliance for Regional Stewardship, he went around the country consulting with and learning from organizations that worked effectively across boundaries for the common good. The most effective regions forge partnerships between the public and private sectors and promote civic engagement by tackling tough community problems together.

Earlier in David's career, when he ran Wharton's Small Business Development Center, he connected the need for entrepreneurial role models in the city's African American community with the University of Pennsylvania's need to strengthen its ties to the surrounding community. His efforts helped launch The Enterprise Center, a minority business accelerator that has been incubating and launching minority businesses for 20 years and now serves as a major economic development force in West Philadelphia under the leadership of Connector Della Clark.

More recently, as head of the Pennsylvania Economy League, David helped launch the Knowledge Industry Partnership, a cross-sector effort to attract and retain college graduates in the region. That effort is now managed by Campus Philly, which is run by Connector Jon Herrmann.

David's understanding of the cultures and key players of each sector have made him one of the most trusted and well-connected professionals in Philadelphia.

Navigating Mazes requires the ability to understand and work through complex organizational structures, both formal and informal. This includes one's own organization, other organizations, and the community.

Connectors know the names and roles of key influencers in their organizations and in their communities. They do not think of others in terms of hierarchies and are not constrained by rank. They know what matters to people at different levels and connect accordingly.

Connectors demonstrate an ability to effectively span traditional organizational boundaries to establish relationships and move plans forward. They demonstrate working knowledge of and insight about other functions and areas of expertise, both inside and outside of one's culture, and draw on this information to develop workable strategies and plans.

Connectors demonstrate awareness of broad community issues that span far beyond the organization within which they operate. They apply their organizational understanding to make decisions that will have the greatest impact and benefit to the community. They demonstrate respect for, interest in, and understanding of the way things get done in sectors other than their own.

SELF ASSESSMENT

Instructions: Please rate yourself on the following behaviors. A (1) means that this is never true of you, while a (5) means that you always do this.

EXERCISE
Are you a Maze Navigator?

1. I work hard at growing and cultivating a diverse network.

1	2	3	4	5
never	rarely	sometimes	usually	always

2. I know how the other parts of my organization work.

1	2	3	4	5
never	rarely	sometimes	usually	always

3. I know the leaders in my community.

1	2	3	4	5
never	rarely	sometimes	usually	always

4. I know the key challenges facing my community.

1	2	3	4	5
never	rarely	sometimes	usually	always

5. I am well read and work to acquire a broad knowledge base.

1	2	3	4	5
never	rarely	sometimes	usually	always

6. I am accessible to colleagues, friends, and acquaintances when they need help solving problems.

1	2	3	4	5
never	rarely	sometimes	usually	always

7. I understand why people do what they do.

1	2	3	4	5
never	rarely	sometimes	usually	always

8. I can and will adjust to the needs and styles of others.

1	2	3	4	5
never	rarely	sometimes	usually	always

9. I have worked in or with people from businesses, government, and non-profit organizations.

1	2	3	4	5
never	rarely	sometimes	usually	always

10. I have developed a wide comfort zone that enables me to relate to a wide range of people.

1	2	3	4	5
never	rarely	sometimes	usually	always

11. I can cut through the details and get to the heart of the problem quickly.

1	2	3	4	5
never	rarely	sometimes	usually	always

12. I attend events hosted by a wide range of organizations.

1	2	3	4	5
never	rarely	sometimes	usually	always

13. I allow members of my team a degree of freedom when solving problems.

1	2	3	4	5
never	rarely	sometimes	usually	always

14. I understand the value of working through informal channels, and I do it well.

1	2	3	4	5
never	rarely	sometimes	usually	always

15. I demonstrate respect and sensitivity when dealing with other cultures.

1	2	3	4	5
never	rarely	sometimes	usually	always

Identify (circle) one behavior to improve in the next year.

Lessons learned from Connectors
about Navigating Mazes

1. Connectors create a network composed of people with different expertise, skill sets, cultural backgrounds, and values. They cultivate this network and tap into it in order to resolve business, community, or social problems.

2. Connectors see great value in becoming familiar with different social and cultural values. They seek out people with differing or opposing values, to whom they listen respectfully. In so doing, they build bridges to others outside of their own function, community, and culture.

3. Connectors engage in systems thinking, understanding that creative problem solving requires a broad range of knowledge, skills, abilities, and perspectives.

4. Connectors pay attention to organizational and community issues, noticing and learning from the different ways that problems are solved.

5. Connectors make themselves accessible to solve problems apparently outside of their expertise. They respond when called to solve problems by people in their network, and are known as "go to" people. They risk venturing into unknown territory to help.

6. Connectors understand and accept different motive patterns in others, and can adjust their behavior and style to fit the style of the other person, and to help the others to fulfill their needs.

7. Connectors practice "code switching" by making subtle surface level changes in communications style and approach in order to develop rapport and a connection with the other person. This fine-tuning does not mean that the Connector's integrity or authenticity is compromised. It is simply a facility with making small changes in conversation that put the other at ease.

8. Connectors are more likely than most to choose to work in different sectors of the economy. Preferring variety over sameness, they enjoy learning how to operate in different organizations. This variety of experience enables them to navigate different cultures and to work with people from other sectors well. Furthermore, the Connector conveys a respect for the uniqueness and complexity of the private, public, and non-profit sectors.

9. Connectors like a wide variety of people and have a wide social comfort zone. They are drawn to people who appear to be different from them, and will reach out to them to learn more. Because they do this with respect, enthusiasm, and with a positive sincere manner, a wide range of people find the Connector to be likeable.

10. Connectors make a conscientious effort to demonstrate interest in other people's work. They ask extensive questions about what someone's job entails, and they create their own memory bank of who does what. They make quick associations and readily identify who can be helpful on a given project.

Behaviors that derail Maze Navigation

1. Deciding to live and work within a very narrow comfort zone. Focusing your efforts solely on your immediate responsibilities at work and at home, without reaching out to connect with and learn from others who are less familiar.

2. Developing deep technical expertise at the expense of developing parallel interpersonal social skills. Becoming so focused on one subject that you are unwilling or unable to carry on conversations on other subjects.

3. Failure to recognize patterns of behavior from the lessons of history.

4. Displaying a lack of interest in other people's work. Keeping social conversations impersonal and superficial (sports/weather/

travel logistics) so that you learn nothing about the people in the conversation. Assuming that others' jobs are less interesting than yours or that others would not be interested in talking about their jobs or yours.

5. Displaying arrogance with a "my way or the highway" approach, leaving others demoralized, disenfranchised, and de-energized.

6. Failing to recognize how much gets done outside of formal channels. Missing the opportunity to access these channels by limiting communication with people like receptionists and assistants, who tend to be the glue that holds organizations together and adept at getting things done.

7. Confining your efforts to work and home without volunteering to help with anything outside (coaching, PTA, faith-related projects, politics, or other civic opportunities).

8. Demonstrating fear of outsiders and limiting your interactions and efforts to people you have known since childhood.

9. Lack of the sensitivity or flexibility to fine tune your behavior to adjust to other organizational cultures within your company or community. Seeing the ability to adjust as a weakness. Failing to understand that integrity is a function of character and deeply held beliefs, not surface level adjustments to put others at ease.

10. Hoarding resources and information from other people or groups so that you are advantaged and they are disadvantaged.

Ten Ways to Navigate Mazes

At work

1. Sign up for cross-functional task forces and project teams. Make it a point to get to know team members from different departments so that you can serve as resources for each other in the future.

2. If it is early in your career, consider taking a job in a sector other than the one you work in now. Choose an assignment in which the client is from another sector. Cultivate friends whose work is different from your own and ask them how their organizations operate.

3. Identify the local hubs of connection across sectors, like the Chamber of Commerce or other places to meet a range of people who care about the community.

4. If your problem solving skills need developing, consider getting an additional technical degree or taking a seminar or two in your area of weakness. If these options are not feasible, find yourself a mentor who is willing to coach you and give you honest feedback. Treat this privilege respectfully, and reach out to your mentor for specific advice.

5. If you sense that your interpersonal skills are lacking, sign up for a reputable course in leadership or emotional intelligence. Get a certified professional to give you the Myers Briggs temperament inventory, and read *Gifts Differing: Understanding Personality Type,* to learn to understand and work with people whose operating style is different from yours.

At home

6. Study and visit different neighborhoods in your community. Dine in their restaurants and participate in their culture festivals. If you have acquaintances from different neighborhoods, invite them to your neighborhood and show them your favorite parts of it. Be a welcoming force in your community.

7. Do a family project on the subject of immigration. Read books and watch movies on the subject together. Have your children study or visit Ellis Island to learn about immigration.

In the community

8. Find out the ethnic origin of your neighborhood and city. Discuss this with your children and take them to the local historic sites to learn more about local cultural history.

9. Join organizations that encourage networking, like Rotary or Kiwanis clubs or Toastmasters. Make an effort to meet several people. Ask them to breakfast or lunch simply to get to know more about each other's work. Send business leads to those contacts and start weaving them into your network.

10. If you work in the private sector, volunteer to do something in the public sector or for a non-profit organization. If you work in the non-profit sector, spend time talking with your private sector board members about their work. If you work in government, spend time learning about the private sector from neighbors and friends who work there.

"The social instinct makes everyone seem like part of a whole, and there is something very appealing about this, because it means that people like Lois Weisberg aren't bound by the same categories and petitions that defeat the rest of us."

Malcolm Gladwell[27]

Empowering Passion

"Enrollment is the art and practice of generating a spark of possibility to share. In the Middle Ages, when lighting a fire from scratch was an arduous process, people often carried about a metal box containing a smoldering cinder, kept alight throughout the day with a little bit of kindling. This meant that a man could light a fire with ease wherever he went, because he always carried the spark."

Rosamund Zander and Benjamin Zander[28]

PAUL VALLAS

Former CEO, School District of Philadelphia;
Current New Orleans Recovery School District Superintendent

Paul Vallas believes in working with a wide range of groups with a wide range of values. "Whatever helps to complete the mission, you work with. You take what's out there and work with it." He brought together a diverse team that reflected the population in the schools and encouraged them to reach out across sectors for help.

Vallas (once a candidate to be the Governor of Illinois) attributes his connecting skills to an early government internship. He learned how to discuss the issues on the "other side of the aisle." When he worked in his father's restaurant, he learned to appreciate a diversity of opinions, to tolerate differences, and to listen to counter conversations. He minored in history and came to understand the "interconnectedness of it all."

Vallas is optimistic about human nature and people's ability to rise up to meet higher expectations. He puts the pressure on to help kids to raise their expectations. In Philadelphia, he worked to create the perception that City kids are college bound, and built schools like the School of the Future to encourage kids to dream big.

Vallas told the following story that illustrated his belief in the power of high expectations. "There was a school in Florida with very poor results. They brought in a new teacher who ended up having extraordinary success with a troubled grade. After a year, his students' performance soared. When asked how this happened, he said that he had inherited an extraordinary class–filled with kids with high IQ scores. His first class list included each student's name and a number, which he had assumed was their IQ score. He later learned that this number was actually each child's locker number. He created the perception that they were extraordinary, so they lived up to it. He communicated that they all have potential and they rose to meet that expectation."

Paul Vallas was called to New Orleans to reinvent the city's school system in the wake of Hurricane Katrina.

Empowering Passion is the genuine desire and ability to create contagious enthusiasm, which inspires others to achieve more than they thought possible.

Connectors assume the best in others. They engage those around them in conversations about possibilities, often linking these possibilities to the common good. They actively spread ideas to others, particularly when these ideas relate to changes that could make a good and positive impact on an organization or the community at large.

Connectors tend to apply their passion in their work. People who love their work radiate an energy that is contagious. They make work seem like play in such a way that others find themselves not only curious about that work, but intrigued by the possibility of joining in on the work. Because they discovered the joy in doing work that they love, they are eager to enroll others in it. They are zealous in helping others to find work that suits them so that others can experience such joy. Optimistic about the possibilities in others, they approach people with enthusiasm and respect.

SELF ASSESSMENT

Instructions: Please rate yourself on the following behaviors. A (1) means that this is never true of you, while a (5) means that you always do this.

EXERCISE
Do you demonstrate Empowering Passion?

1. I show enthusiasm for my own ideas and the ideas of others.

1	2	3	4	5
never	rarely	sometimes	usually	always

2. I get others excited about doing something for the common good.

1	2	3	4	5
never	rarely	sometimes	usually	always

3. People use the word "energetic" to describe me.

1	2	3	4	5
never	rarely	sometimes	usually	always

4. I give speeches that get people excited about and engaged in my work or theirs.

1	2	3	4	5
never	rarely	sometimes	usually	always

5. I approach people at work expecting positive things of them.

1	2	3	4	5
never	rarely	sometimes	usually	always

6. I make it a point to make eye contact with people I encounter.

1	2	3	4	5
never	rarely	sometimes	usually	always

7. I am committed to helping others succeed.

1	2	3	4	5
never	rarely	sometimes	usually	always

8. I strive to be a role model at work and/or at home and/or in the community.

1	2	3	4	5
never	rarely	sometimes	usually	always

9. People tell me that I have inspired them to do better or more.

1	2	3	4	5
never	rarely	sometimes	usually	always

10. I make an effort to help younger people with career issues.

1	2	3	4	5
never	rarely	sometimes	usually	always

11. I am willing to share my own failures and lessons learned.

1	2	3	4	5
never	rarely	sometimes	usually	always

12. I nominate others for awards and recognition.

1	2	3	4	5
never	rarely	sometimes	usually	always

13. I ask people about their hopes and dreams.

1	2	3	4	5
never	rarely	sometimes	usually	always

14. I think about the needs of my community and what I can do to fulfill them.

1	2	3	4	5
never	rarely	sometimes	usually	always

15. People come to me to find out what's going on in the community.

1	2	3	4	5
never	rarely	sometimes	usually	always

Identify (circle) one behavior to improve in the next year.

Lessons learned from Connectors
about Empowering Passion

1. Connectors demonstrate a type of coaching mentality when working with others. They find ways to help others succeed and take pride in making others look good. The person who is being coached can tell that the coach is invested in his/her development and strives to succeed in part to repay that investment.

2. Connectors often experience their work as a calling. They are on a mission, and their belief in it gives others something to believe in. This sense of purpose and drive is obvious to those around them, who are drawn to be part of the action.

3. Connectors rally others around their plans by creating a compelling picture of the future, which is exciting, yet feasible. Robert Cross and Andrew Parker capture this notion beautifully in *The Hidden Power of Social Networks* as follows:

   > Energy lives in a sweet spot in five dimensions of conversations or group problem solving sessions: a compelling goal; the possibility of contributing; a strong sense of engagement; the perception of progress, and the belief that the idea can succeed.[29]

4. Connectors energize others in conversation. They do this by expressing enthusiasm for what they are doing and then turning the focus to the other person to express enthusiasm for what that person is doing. They ask questions of the other to encourage that person to think about what is going well in his or her life. Connectors ask about the other's successes, and express enthusiasm and specific praise for the other's contribution. People often reach out to Connectors when they need pep talks. Olympic hockey coach Herb Brooks did this for people, as author Ross Bernstein recalls. "Every time I would see him, I would just get such a shot of adrenaline. Just seeing him gave me such a rush."[30]

5. Connectors demonstrate an optimism that gives others hope. They strive to keep conversations upbeat and look for ways to

help others focus on what is right about a situation, rather than what is wrong. They subtly switch the topic away from barriers, obstacles, and other depressing ways of framing subjects. While they acknowledge that these obstacles and setbacks are valid, they don't allow the conversations to get unduly negative, but rather offer specific, realistic possibilities to contemplate as alternatives.

6. In what used to be considered simply good manners, Connectors seize opportunities to create positive moments with others. They say good morning or good afternoon in elevators, they make eye contact, and smile at strangers, and say hello to people they pass on the streets. They ask for things in a tone that acknowledges to the other that they will be grateful for the help. When they call someone, they are cognizant of the other's frame of mind and ask, "Is this a good time to talk?" As mundane as these practices sound, they are sufficiently rare that others take note, if only for an instant, that the Connector noticed them.

7. Connectors work to move the conversation away from "no" toward "yes." Comedians learn this behavior when they learn improvisation. To keep the flow going, they find a way to affirm what the other person just said and thus move the story forward. If you observe good improvisation, you are seeing Connection as an art form. A story-line moves forward and gains momentum as others add to it in a positive way. The players energize the audience with the clever way that they escalate the situation, and the audience energizes the players with their grateful applause. In more subtle fashion, Connectors lift the conversation in such a way that the other feels the multiplier effect of their uplifting connection.

8. Connectors actively spread ideas to others wherever possible, particularly ideas that relate to broad and positive changes in the organization or community. They initiate conversations about these ideas with the conviction that the other person will probably benefit from knowing the ideas. Because they are so excited about being "in the know," they project their excitement on others and share new information in an open and animated fashion.

Connectors initiate such conversations assuming that the person across the table would find the topic fascinating. Unlike those who lack their skill set, however, Connectors are so attuned to others' reactions that they change the subject as soon as they detect a lack of interest on the others' part.

9. Connectors create opportunities for others to get more involved in their communities or causes. Unable to contain their enthusiasm, they set up and attend meetings where they sense an opportunity to engage others. They understand the need to inform others of what is required to make positive changes in the community and they take the initiative to create opportunities for positive discussions around such possibilities.

10. Connectors actively gather diverse opinions on community issues in order to be prepared to have open, inclusive and productive discussions of community issues. They not only engage in civic discourse, but encourage friends and acquaintances to do so by providing venues, facts, and welcoming settings that promote open discussion and shared understanding.

Behaviors that derail Empowering Passion

1. Carrying on conversations that focus on what is wrong rather than what is right. Allowing the topic to spiral into a series of negative views, thus pulling both parties down a worst-case scenario path.

2. Allowing yourself to get so overwhelmed with professional and personal obligations that you have no capacity to open up to others about their issues.

3. Entering into conversations in which your sole focus is getting what you want. Being so intent on achieving your goals that you fail to show any interest in the other person, thereby leaving them feeling used and unexcited about the prospect of future meetings with you.

4. Displaying a "keeping score" mentality by entering relationships or interactions assuming that the exchange of information or goodwill must be even. Connectors are willing to give more than they receive in a given interaction. People who lack Connector skills may end up feeling cheated by others when a specific exchange is not equal. Others perceive the lack of generosity in such exchanges and put their guard up in subsequent exchanges to avoid being used. A reputation for being generous gets your call returned.

5. Using intimidation and being overly reliant on rank may get conformity but does not engender the kind of loyalty and receptivity enjoyed by Connectors. Signaling that the other person must do something simply because you outrank them may result in getting the task done. If this is the only tool in your toolkit, however, you will miss the added leverage of bringing out the best in people by treating your interactions as mutual.

6. Working with closed agendas and plans with no input from others squelches their initiative and buy-in. Failing to elicit and consider others' suggestions deprives them of developmental opportunities and reduces the likelihood of exploring all possibilities and creative options. This micromanaging mentality decreases the energy of the team.

7. Demonstrating a lack of interest in the hopes and dreams of those around you denies you the opportunity to help them to realize their hopes and denies them the benefit of your advice and counsel. Since others will usually keep these dreams to themselves unless asked, failing to extend that invitation is a missed opportunity for both parties.

8. Many people are so overwhelmed with their professional and personal obligations that they shut down and try to keep their world small and controlled. They don't watch the news because it has too many negative stories, or they say they are too busy to read the newspaper. This form of self-imposed isolation, while understandable, squelches community involvement and decreases the likelihood that neighbors will help one another.

9. Lack of self-awareness prevents some people from connecting. They may not know, for instance, that others find them dismissive or unidimensional or difficult to connect with. Failure to make an investment in knowing how others experience you limits your opportunities to interact with the widest possible range of interesting people whose lives you may enrich, or who may be of help to you.

10. Treating the people you meet as transactions is the opposite of connection. If you signal—subtly or not so subtly—that you are a short-timer for whatever reason, be prepared to be the social equivalent of a political lame duck.

Ten Ways to develop Empowering Passion

At work

1. Commit to being a positive voice for the work that you do. If it is a project, identify, emphasize, and reinforce its merit. If you are involved in a merger, think and talk about the positive outcomes. Act like an optimist and build a reputation for optimism.

2. Identify your most positive and enthusiastic colleagues and staff members. Give them specific positive feedback in public and in private. Document examples of their impact and take every opportunity to reinforce positive behavior and discourage nay-saying.

3. Commit to mining for the gold in younger employees. Take an active interest in their progress and help get them exposure and opportunities. Target promising younger employees and support their careers. Take them to lunch to discuss their interests and plans, and find ways to help them succeed.

4. Speak up to the nay-sayers and counter their negative comments with appropriate positive perceptions. Do not reinforce or promote employees whose attitudes are toxic to their colleagues.

At home

5. Focus on what your kids do well and take every opportunity to give them specific positive feedback when they deserve it. This must be genuine and concrete in order to be motivating to them. Identify 2-3 things that each of your children is good at or enthusiastic about. Pay attention to what they do in those areas and give them positive feedback when they earn it.

6. Create a culture of optimism in your home. Lead discussions about what is right in the world and what is inspiring in your community. Encourage your children to talk about the positive attributes of their friends, teammates, family members and other contacts. Discourage excessive criticism or any teasing.

7. Pay attention to the neighborhood kids and your kids' friends. Treat them as individuals and find time to talk to them about their interests. Encourage them with specific positive feedback. If they have a setback or seem discouraged, spend time listening to and sitting with them. When you sense that they are ready to be helped, give them alternative ways to solve their problem.

In the community

8. Practice paying it forward and performing random acts of kindness. Make it your goal to improve the quality of someone's day. Be vigilant for ways to help or serve someone. See www.payitforwardfoundation.com for ideas. Listen carefully for the needs of others. If someone can't find a book or a reference, take the time to find it for them. Your act can range from helping an elderly person with heavy bags at the store to shoveling a neighbor's driveway, to any range of good deeds.

9. Adopt a class of a school or a congregation that needs supplies or other assistance. Make yourself available to assist in small but useful ways. Be vigilant in identifying ways to serve. Volunteer to spend time with elders in a local nursing home. Ask them about their families and interests and share your stories.

10. Volunteer to help a local cultural institution by bringing friends to events or supporting the work of the artists. By all means donate funds if you can, but also donate time and contacts.

"Where others at that level might come in with preconceived plans and totally ignore your work, she [a Connector] always comes in open and willing to listen to what you have done. She shows a value for your effort and ideas that makes you want to do your best then and later."

Robert L. Cross and Andrew Parker[31]

Constantly Curious

"Where does this font of uncommon knowledge come from? [A Connector] engages in 'pointless networking'—lunches, breakfasts, and meetings that have no perceptible agenda. If she reads about a person whom she finds interesting, she introduces herself, suggests that they get acquainted, and usually acquires a friend (or at least a new source of information). She's not devious or manipulative; she's just curious. She finds different people interesting and seeks them out from a broad range of industries, levels, and callings."

Douglas B. Richardson[32]

PHIL GOLDSMITH
*Former City Managing Director, Head of Fairmount Park,
and CEO, Philadelphia School District*

Phil Goldsmith is Philadelphia's version of the late George Plimpton—on steroids. His competence, commitment, confidence, and curiosity have mobilized him to serve in a wide range of key leadership positions. An attorney by training, he started in the Justice Department in Harrisburg and ran the Philadelphia Bar Association. He worked for the *Morning Call* newspaper in Allentown and as a journalist for *The Philadelphia Inquirer,* where he was a Pulitzer Prize finalist. He was a senior executive with PNC Bank, a local search firm and a national outplacement business. In government he worked on Bill Green's Mayoral campaign, served as a deputy mayor, School District CEO, head of Fairmount Park, and City Managing Director. Currently he is a consultant in and leader of efforts to stop gun violence in Pennsylvania.

When explaining his behavior as a Connector, Phil says, "I've had the opportunity to work in a number of different fields. I've met a lot of people in different boxes. I'm better thinking horizontally than vertically. Most concepts are the same—the jargon is just different across sectors. As a result of doing this stuff I see the interrelationships between things. I can translate others' challenges and relate to them." He also mentions these actions:

- "I specifically put people together and bow out."
- "I like to meet new people; I embarrass my kids because I talk to everyone. It floors me how many times I make a connection."
- "I'm intellectually curious. I like stories."
- "I'm a strong believer that we have to get out of our silos."
- "I'm accessible and am eager to meet with people."
- "I understand that people can be helpful to each other even though they don't know how yet, and that help may happen 20 years later."
- "I understand individual perspectives—that people are not good or bad, they just occupy a different perch. I understand their perch."

Phil's trademark is his willingness to step into tough jobs at critical times. His curiosity has opened doors for him and moved major organizations forward. This lifelong learner builds bridges between groups and creates community by connecting.

Constantly Curious people are lifelong learners who work continuously to expand their perspective and experience.

Connectors demonstrate intellectual as well as interpersonal curiosity. They ask questions to fully understand issues and people. They willingly take things on about which they have limited knowledge. They actively seek out situations, people and information to support this quest.

Connectors are drawn to variety over sameness. They have a wide and permeable comfort zone that allows them to interact effectively with people from different backgrounds and points of view. They help others to bridge their differences by identifying and articulating what they have in common.

Connectors engage others in dialogues to resolve small differences before those differences interfere with achieving a broader goal of mutual interest. This happens because they set a tone and create processes which allow all views to be aired and heard as part of the decision-making process.

Operating on the world-view that everything is connected, Connectors create opportunities for others to acquire this viewpoint by exposing others to diverse perspectives. They consciously advocate for inclusion by convening diverse groups of people to discuss or resolve community challenges and to celebrate the richness of diverse perspectives.

SELF ASSESSMENT

Instructions: Please rate yourself on the following behaviors. A (1) means that this is never true of you, while a (5) means that you always do this.

EXERCISE
Do you demonstrate Constant Curiosity?

1. I am excited by the prospect of meeting someone new, particularly if they are different from me in some obvious way.

1	2	3	4	5
never	rarely	sometimes	usually	always

2. I sign up for seminars that will broaden my knowledge.

1	2	3	4	5
never	rarely	sometimes	usually	always

3. I learn new and interesting things from acquaintances.

1	2	3	4	5
never	rarely	sometimes	usually	always

4. I believe that everyone has something valuable to teach others.

1	2	3	4	5
never	rarely	sometimes	usually	always

5. I make an effort to bring together people with different backgrounds and viewpoints.

1	2	3	4	5
never	rarely	sometimes	usually	always

6. I force myself to widen my comfort zone to continue to grow.

1	2	3	4	5
never	rarely	sometimes	usually	always

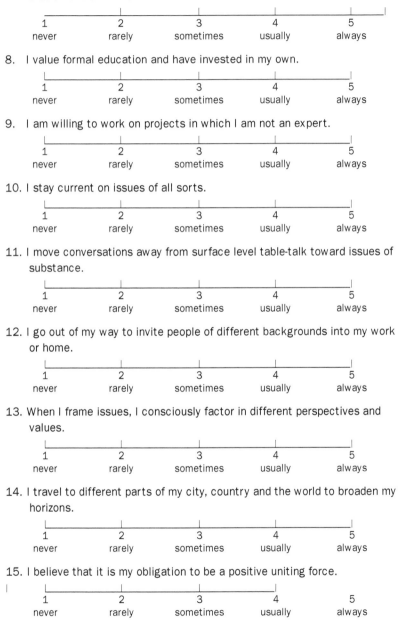

7. I read articles and watch or listen to shows that come from perspectives that differ from mine.

1	2	3	4	5
never	rarely	sometimes	usually	always

8. I value formal education and have invested in my own.

1	2	3	4	5
never	rarely	sometimes	usually	always

9. I am willing to work on projects in which I am not an expert.

1	2	3	4	5
never	rarely	sometimes	usually	always

10. I stay current on issues of all sorts.

1	2	3	4	5
never	rarely	sometimes	usually	always

11. I move conversations away from surface level table-talk toward issues of substance.

1	2	3	4	5
never	rarely	sometimes	usually	always

12. I go out of my way to invite people of different backgrounds into my work or home.

1	2	3	4	5
never	rarely	sometimes	usually	always

13. When I frame issues, I consciously factor in different perspectives and values.

1	2	3	4	5
never	rarely	sometimes	usually	always

14. I travel to different parts of my city, country and the world to broaden my horizons.

1	2	3	4	5
never	rarely	sometimes	usually	always

15. I believe that it is my obligation to be a positive uniting force.

1	2	3	4	5
never	rarely	sometimes	usually	always

Identify (circle) one behavior that you will improve next year.

Lessons on Constant Curiosity learned from Connectors

1. Connectors seek truth rather than validation of their own opinions. They do this by formally studying other approaches, disciplines or cultures. They are energized by the process of acquiring knowledge.

2. Connectors treat other people as subjects to be studied. They ask questions about others' experience, education, culture, and beliefs in such a way that the other opens up and shares freely. Connectors express gratitude for the privilege of learning more about another's life.

3. Connectors frequently demonstrate a range of professional experience. They may have worked in several organizations or industries and enjoyed getting to know a range of technologies, corporate cultures, and operating styles. In so doing they have taught themselves to fit into a range of different settings.

4. Connectors delight in learning about others' jobs. They practically interview new friends and acquaintances to learn what they do. The more different the others' experience, the more excited Connectors get, for this new knowledge broadens their inventory of information to share with others when it is needed in the future.

5. Connectors feel restless with too much routine at work or at home, so they go out of their way to seek the stimulation of the new. They volunteer for new projects or take on new home improvement or adventure travel projects to broaden their perspective or experience.

6. Connectors are not content to hoard information. They feel that the value of information increases when you share it. When they learn something new, they contact someone else who they think will value it, and share the information. They love to "show and tell" at work and at home, so are constantly injecting new information into their social circle.

7. Connectors set aside time to meet new people and to learn new things. While others feel overwhelmed by being busy, connectors prefer to be fully engaged, and will therefore make room for a new encounter if they see it as a learning opportunity.

8. Connectors seek the stimulation of collaborating. They like to have their ideas challenged by people who are also open to listening and learning. They enjoy observing the decision making process, and they track the way ideas unfold during a meeting or conversation. They can articulate this unfolding to others in such a way that they not only know that their viewpoint was considered, but how and why it did or did not fit the solution.

9. Connectors are comfortable with ambiguity. Confident of their own problem-solving skills and curious to learn others' points of view, they love to watch the puzzle come together. Their prior experience, willingness to risk, and faith that a practical solution can be found allow them to engage in a range of problem-solving activities.

10. Connectors actively seek opportunities to brainstorm with others. They are often sought out by others who need to think through big problems or decisions that are complicated and may fall into the gray area of breaking new ground. They value their creative side and are energized in the presence of other creative people. They are drawn to fields that require innovation. They are driven to keep current.

Behaviors that derail Constant Curiosity

1. Acting on the assumption that you already know everything you need to know. This includes believing there is only one way to do something or to think about something.

2. Closing your mind to the possibility that there are valid beliefs besides your own; assuming that people who think, act, or feel differently are wrong and you are right.

3. Dismissing issues as simple. Failing to look at the nuances or complexity or richness of issues and people. Seeking comfort in having yes/no answers on every issue. Showing discomfort with solutions "in the gray area."

4. Limiting your interests to a narrow range of subjects. Failing to attempt to learn about things or beliefs you did not learn inside your own home or from your family and friends. Believing that what you have learned in your closed social circle is all you need to know to succeed.

5. Failing to familiarize yourself with the positions of the political party you do not support. Likewise failing to learn about countries whose cultures or governments differ from those of the United States.

6. Avoiding or ignoring the lessons of history. Failing to grasp the importance of lessons learned from former leaders and conflicts. Assuming that contemporary problems bear no relationship to historic events.

7. Ignoring technological advances and assuming that they are too difficult or time consuming to learn. Operating without the benefits of technological advances.

8. Avoiding meetings, events, gatherings, or parties where you don't know many people. Assuming that these situations will be awkward, useless, and a waste of your time.

9. Missing opportunities to showcase colleagues, staff, students, children, or friends with different viewpoints, knowledge, or skill sets. Assuming that people only want to meet others like themselves, and assembling teams and events accordingly.

10. Hiding behind a heavy workload to avoid new experiences and people. Assuming that you are too busy to add one more responsibility or encounter to your life. Using work as an excuse to avoid socializing.

Ten ways to encourage Constant Curiosity

At work

1. Take time periodically during staff meetings to ask each person at the table to share something that interests them outside of work.

2. Hold an annual offsite staff meeting that includes specific exercises designed to help you to get to know each other better. Instead of having social time consisting of bar chatter, make an effort to organize structured conversations, with the goal of knowing each other better by the end of the session.

3. Encourage employees to take advantage of education benefits. Determine who needs to complete degrees and encourage them to do so. Encourage your employees to attend seminars inside and outside of work and to report back to colleagues what they learned. Rotate people through other departments to broaden their perspectives.

4. Consider taking a job in another industry or technical specialty. Think about areas of interest that you have never pursued and find people in those fields to talk to about their jobs. Take courses to prepare yourself for a shift of jobs or accountabilities.

At home

5. Take time during dinner to learn something interesting from each person at the table. Call on each person and do not let them take a "pass." Give them equal air time, even if that requires using an hourglass or a timer.

6. Pick a subject for your family to focus on for a month. This can be related to the interest of a family member or a project due for work or for school. Assign different age-appropriate investigations on the topic so everyone contributes to a discussion about it at the end of the month. Visit a related site or look it up on the Internet or

in the library. This can range from kittens to the Kremlin–simply explore together to model curiosity for your kids.

7. Identify three museums to visit as a family this year. Find out what the options are in your city, and make it a point to see all of them over time. Bring home brochures and talk about what you saw, what you learned, and what else it makes you want to explore.

In your community

8. Sign up for a class in local history. Find out about the roots of your home and your neighborhood. What kind of people have lived there? What businesses were there and are there now? Where did its name come from? Who founded it? Who or what are the roads named after and why?

9. Visit your state capital. Take a tour to learn more about state history. Bring your kids along. Move on to the local historical society to learn about the way your state's population and economy grew. Read more about some aspect of its founding, growth, demographics, or economy that interest you. Talk about age-appropriate related topics with your kids.

10. Visit Washington, D.C. Arrange to tour the White House and Congress. Have your children look up information on your Senators and Representatives, and arrange to stop by one of their offices. Visit the Smithsonian to see national treasures and other points of interest to you and your children. Write a thank you note to an elected official and have your children do the same.

"I have no special talents. I am only passionately curious."

Albert Einstein

Trustworthy

"In the end, all you have is your reputation."

Oprah Winfrey

CHARISSE R. LILLIE

Vice President of Community Investment, Comcast Corporation
Executive Vice President of the Comcast Foundation

If you were to ask professionals in Philadelphia to list the local role models for integrity, the name Charisse Lillie would be near or at the top of most lists. An attorney by trade, Charisse worked in the Civil Rights Division of the Department of Justice, Community Legal Services, taught at Villanova University School of Law, served as Philadelphia's City Solicitor, and was a partner and Chair of Litigation at Ballard Spahr. Subsequently, she joined Comcast's corporate staff, working with fellow Connector and former Ballard partner, David L. Cohen. She is a former chair of the board of the Federal Reserve Bank of Philadelphia and has played a leadership role on many non-profit boards, including LEADERSHIP Philadelphia, the Juvenile Law Center, Friends Select School and Howard University.

With Charisse, what you see is what you get. She wears no corporate mask. The Charisse you meet at Comcast is the Charisse you see at home. Both commanding and warm, Charisse has the presence and wit of her fellow Texan, the late Senator Barbara Jordan, who was also known for her integrity. Charisse is very approachable, and her gentle logical approach overlies a fierce intellect and long-standing commitment to diversity. When asked about her accomplishments, Lillie mentions the increased diversity in her firm and in the local legal community. Her integrity and effective approach helped to put this issue into national debate.

When asked about specific Connector behaviors, Charisse says that she is:

- "optimistic and attuned to others."
- "a student of human persistence."
- "honest and trustworthy."
- "eager to hear the truth, even if it hurts."
- "quick to trust, but if lied to, it's a long road back."
- "very attached to her friends, including friends from first grade."
- "careful to send hand written notes and birthday cards."
- "committed to philanthropy and giving back to her institutions in order to stay connected."
- "actively engaged in mentoring and serving as a role model."

This committed executive has succeeded in modeling integrity and trustworthiness to the colleagues and community members who share the good fortune of working with and knowing her.

Trustworthy people keep their word, demonstrate integrity, and stay true to their values.

Connectors are seen as "the real deal." With them, what you see is what you get. They wear no social mask and tend to behave at home as they do at work. Their behavior is consistent and reliable over time so that those around them can count on their judgment, discretion, and results. Others find comfort in their integrity, reliability, and accountability, so they often seek them out in times of crisis or for help in making decisions.

SELF ASSESSMENT

Instructions: Please rate yourself on the following behaviors. A (1) means that you never do this, while a (5) means that this is always true of you.

Exercise
Are you Trustworthy?

1. I share information appropriately and on a timely basis.

1	2	3	4	5
never	rarely	sometimes	usually	always

2. I have a reputation for following through on commitments.

1	2	3	4	5
never	rarely	sometimes	usually	always

3. With me, what you see is what you get.

1	2	3	4	5
never	rarely	sometimes	usually	always

4. I am seen as someone who can take a tough stand.

1	2	3	4	5
never	rarely	sometimes	usually	always

5. People think of me as someone who keeps confidences.

1	2	3	4	5
never	rarely	sometimes	usually	always

6. Others seek my advice when they need help.

1	2	3	4	5
never	rarely	sometimes	usually	always

7. I'm essentially the same at work as I am at home.

1	2	3	4	5
never	rarely	sometimes	usually	always

8. I believe that I make a difference.

1	2	3	4	5
never	rarely	sometimes	usually	always

9. Being trustworthy is one of my highest values.

1	2	3	4	5
never	rarely	sometimes	usually	always

10. I am conscious of my ethical and moral obligations to others.

1	2	3	4	5
never	rarely	sometimes	usually	always

11. I demonstrate self-control and stay composed even when I am angry.

1	2	3	4	5
never	rarely	sometimes	usually	always

12. When I make mistakes, I apologize and I mean it.

1	2	3	4	5
never	rarely	sometimes	usually	always

13. I carry my weight and am seen as a team player.

1	2	3	4	5
never	rarely	sometimes	usually	always

14. Others can count on me to be reliable and responsible.

1	2	3	4	5
never	rarely	sometimes	usually	always

15. I factor the common good into my decisions.

1	2	3	4	5
never	rarely	sometimes	usually	always

Identify (circle) one behavior to improve in the next year.

Lessons learned from Connectors about being Trustworthy

1. Connectors share information liberally and on a timely basis. They are proactive about bringing people into the fold and give thought to who should be brought into the conversation. If they see an article or hear of something that would be useful to someone else, they take a few extra minutes to send a note or to pick up the phone to share the information. Furthermore, they don't delay in getting back to someone who calls. They show a sense of urgency in sharing information.

2. Connectors can be counted on to follow through on their commitments again and again, year after year. This behavior is consistent from work to play. If they say they'll meet a deadline, they will. If they say they'll show up for their child's soccer game, they will, no matter what obstacles they have to overcome. Connectors hold themselves and others accountable and place a high value on their duty to others.

3. Connectors, while tactful, say what they mean and mean what they say. They are direct and to the point in conversations, neither pulling punches when something needs to be said, nor unduly sugar-coating bad news. They are known for having no hidden agenda and for being "straight shooters." Others need not waste time trying to figure out what the Connector really meant, because Connectors speak clearly, carefully, and concisely. Furthermore, they often check for understanding to ensure that everyone heard the message clearly.

4. Connectors take unpopular stands if they feel very strongly about an issue. They make their views known diplomatically, but clearly. They listen to all sides of the issue, and are willing to stand firm for a strongly held position, even if they stand alone. Even in this minority position, the Connector will express respect for and understanding of the opposing or majority view. They are simply willing to draw a line in the sand on some issues, respecting others' right to do the same. They are willing to "agree to disagree." Others can count on them to take a stand.

5. Connectors demonstrate discretion. Others are willing to share information with them freely, because Connectors have a reputation for handling confidences carefully. Connectors demonstrate a non-judgmental receptivity that causes others to feel safe sharing information that they would not feel comfortable sharing with others. The Connector's attentive look, quiet nodding, and patience in letting the speaker tell his tale invites others to be candid and open.

6. Connectors demonstrate comfort in talking to others in crisis. Because they do not have rigid boundaries between different facets of their life, they are willing to let others talk to them about serious professional or personal problems. Either the Connector has weathered storms personally, or has been in so many serious conversations, that he or she has a broad tolerance for crisis related topics and some value to add from his/her or others' related experience. Because the Connector sits still and listens, knowing that simply listening may be more important than problem-solving at that moment, others calm down enough to gather their thoughts and unburden, trusting that they have found a sympathetic ear and may get good advice.

7. Connectors strive to be ethical, honest, and authentic with others. They are known to have a strong moral compass, and others count on them to behave accordingly. They act as if they are role models for others and strive to set a good example, even when they know no one is looking. They speak up when they feel a solution lacks integrity. They avoid dealing with people whose ethics are questionable, even when that means missing out on opportunities and advantages. Others view Connectors as anchors for this reason.

8. Connectors project confidence in their ability to make a difference. Operating from a high level of self-awareness, they know their strengths and weaknesses. They are willing to admit their weaknesses to teams they are on by gathering people who are stronger than them in their weak areas. Conversely, they own their strengths and feel comfortable demonstrating them. For example,

if their life experience has shown them to be resilient in the face of adversity, they step up and try other things at which they may fail, confident that they can overcome failure. Their past successes lead them to believe that they will succeed in the future. They believe in themselves in such a way that others believe in them too.

9. Connectors approach others with respect, withholding judgment and giving them the opportunity to express themselves. Their world view holds the belief that everyone has something to contribute and deserves a chance. They actually have an affinity for the underdog and cheer most loudly when the underdog wins. Either through good manners, faith, or a deep sense of justice, Connectors treat others fairly. They begin by trusting others and continue to do so until proven wrong.

10. Connectors demonstrate integrity. Their standards for respect, access, manners, and accountability are constant from one setting to the next. What you see is what you get with a Connector. They treat the janitor with the same respect and courtesy that they show the CEO. Their demeanor is consistent so that others gain comfort in finding Connectors to be predictable and stable. Connectors strive to be genuine and authentic in their dealings with others.

Behaviors that derail Trust

11. Remaining silent about strongly held beliefs when ethical dilemmas arise. Being known to look the other way when others close by step over ethical boundaries.

12. Expressing anger and frustration in such a way that others shut down and cease trying to make their case when it differs from yours.

13. Blaming others for mistakes and shortcomings, rather than facing up to your own role in the problem. Failing to see or acknowledge to others that you have done something wrong. Not apologizing for it and trying to get the situation back on track.

14. Saying one thing and meaning another. Operating with a hidden agenda, pretending to be a team player with little intention of helping others.

15. Acting only to further your own self-interest. Ignoring or being blind to the needs of the whole. Gathering ideas and resources with no intention of sharing, reciprocating or contributing to the greater good.

16. Focusing on style over substance (in yourself and others.) Spending more time on packaging than content so that something looks good, but may not function well. This approval-seeking behavior may work in the short run with others who share this value. It does not work in the long run with people of substance.

17. Flip-flopping and taking stands that are seen as unpredictable and inconsistent. Demonstrating a lack of attachment to ideals, leaving others afraid to align with you or feeling confused about your motives and beliefs.

18. Treating others as transactions, and merely as a means to your ends. Behaving in an impersonal manner with others who are not immediately useful to you. Dismissing people outside of your inner circle as useless. Showing little or no interest in others' concerns.

19. Failing to deliver on promises. Over-promising, hoping to deliver but knowing at some level that you probably can't do what you said you could do. Missing deadlines without warning others. Raising others' expectations beyond what you know you can deliver.

20. Holding yourself to high standards at work (delivering results; keeping your word; and being punctual), while consistently failing to meet these standards at home or with friends. Letting yourself off the hook when it comes to personal obligations. Treating appointments with friends and families as postponable and dispensable if something better comes up.

Ten Ways to Build Trustworthiness

At work

1. Share information: Some people find comfort in hoarding information, believing that knowledge is power. Connectors, on the other hand, believe that sharing information results in better outcomes. Be vigilant about identifying who needs to be included in meetings. This includes keeping your staff informed of the big picture context in which they operate.

2. Take employees to lunch: New employees tend to flounder silently when they first enter organizations. They wait to be invited to lunches and meetings as they work to learn the culture. Reach out to someone new in your organization to invite them to lunch and share useful information: who are the key executives, what are the organization's priorities, and what are the basics of how people succeed. Let them know that someone noticed them and cares.

3. Keep confidences: Be willing to listen to a colleague's concerns. Make it your business to know something about their children and to ask how they are, or even how you might help them. If you see an opportunity to do a favor for them, do it. Share some basic information about your family and look for common ground. Keep your door open and be willing to spend some time understanding others' family context and to share your own.

At home

4. Identify one concrete way to connect with your spouse/significant other around an interest of theirs. Schedule recreation/social events with the same level of discipline as you use on your office calendar. Work on being fully present at home. Discipline yourself to confine office calls and work to specific hours in a specific place in your home. Do not let work interfere with family meals, vacations, or driving time. Create similar boundaries for the kids,

emphasizing the importance of really being there for each other and connecting while you are together.

5. Reinforce ethics and integrity: Make every effort to comment on your children's integrity and trustworthiness. When they demonstrate this—even on a small scale—give them positive feedback. You can also write a short note commending them on the specific act. Also, comment on report card remarks or on good sportsmanship. Start family conversations around the subject of trust and integrity. Encourage each family member to share examples. Reinforce this as a family value on every possible occasion.

6. Honor your time commitments: Too often we take our personal time for granted, feeling that an hour or two late here and there won't matter. Actually, it matters a great deal to the person or people whose plans are inconvenienced by your tardiness. If you do this too often, your partner or children will not trust your word about scheduling and may become resentful or dismissive of you. Work on being careful about scheduling meetings around critical family deadlines (birthday celebrations, key games, carpool). Each time you miss a deadline, take note and make amends in some real way to the person involved.

7. Stand up for a cause: Commit your energy to the common good. Identify an issue you are passionate about. Look for a community organization that includes that subject in their mission. Contact the organization and volunteer to help in some way. If you don't know where to start, contact your local United Way, community leadership organization, or house of worship for suggestions.

In the community

8. Broaden your perspective: Read the newspaper. If you feel strongly—either for or against an issue—send a letter to the Editor. Be specific about your reaction. If it is negative, suggest a productive alternative in the body of the letter. Learn both sides of issues so you can engage in respectful and informed conversation.

9. Go to a public meeting: Attend local public township or civic organization meetings. Consider this to be your continuing education, and make it your business to understand the infrastructure and issues of your town. Introduce yourself to fellow community members. Learn about their concerns and capabilities and share yours.

10. Thank public servants for jobs well done: Find out more about your local elected officials and first responders. Learn about their issues and needs. If something moves you, volunteer to help or send a contribution. When you observe or hear about something they have done well, send them a letter of appreciation.

[I learned from him how] "to be a man of character. . . . If your word means anything, then when you shake someone's hand, you look them in the eye and say what is in your heart. Then you don't need a contract; you live by your word."

Hockey player Bill Butters, about
Olympic hockey coach Herb Brooks
(subject of the movie *Miracle*)[33]

Optimistic

"This new leader carries the distinction that it is the framework of fear and scarcity, not scarcity itself, that promotes divisions between people. . . . This leader calls upon our passion rather than our fear."

Rosamund Zander and Benjamin Zander[34]

JANE GOLDEN
Executive Director, Philadelphia's Mural Arts Program

Jane Golden is on a mission. For the past 25 years, she has been the heart and engine behind the Mural Arts Program, a unique hybrid of city agency and nonprofit organization that has educated over 20,000 underserved youth while creating more than 3,000 murals. These compelling works of art have become an integral part of the civic landscape and a source of inspiration to the thousands of residents and visitors who encounter them each year.

A veritable force of nature, Jane often refers to herself as a "pest" when describing her relentless efforts to gain funding from the city to complement the private donations she raises for community projects, art education programs, and prison outreach.

The murals created by Jane and her team might not stand apart from other public art if it were not for the social justice, community revitalization, and civic engagement campaigns that inspire them. The murals give neighborhoods hope, often bringing beauty into places where it is absent and engaging neighbors in dialogue that is hard to spark. One of Golden's battle cries—"I won't take no for an answer!"—is a signature trait of the kind of tenacious optimism that she embodies.

Driven by a commitment to heartfelt principles she developed during her involvement with public art beginning in the early '80s, Jane employs a range of tactics to do what she feels is right. She and other Connectors like her don't wait to be invited into a process and don't give up. Not only does Jane achieve a social impact that far outweighs her limited funds, but she does so in spite of fighting a personal battle with the illness Lupus. She is simply too focused and driven to give in to an illness that immobilizes so many of its victims.

Jane's respectful demeanor and strong listening skills allow her to make strides with citizens and within neighborhoods that others have abandoned or ignored. Her work has led to improved race relations and fostered cultural understanding throughout many of the City's neighborhoods. Her groundbreaking efforts in the areas of art education and prisoner rehabilitation and re-entry have earned international recognition. She sees possibilities where others would see futility, mobilizing her staff and artists, along with city agencies, nonprofit organizations, community leaders and residents to build positive communities and create art that empowers all who see it.

In honor of the Mural Arts Program's 25th Anniversary, Jane's team recently completed the "This We Believe" city-wide mural project in conjunction with LEADERSHIP Philadelphia's 50th Anniversary "This I Believe" series produced with WHYY radio. The Mural Arts Program facilitated community meetings in the spring, gathering citizens from every corner of the Philadelphia to find out what they believe about themselves, their neighbors, and their City. Two teams of muralists listened to these stories and produced two designs from the raw material of the community process. The final mural design was selected by a public vote. This inclusive, democratic process is the ultimate realization of Jane's love for and confidence in the communities she serves, the power she sees in the smallest window of possibility, and her drive to overcome profound struggles to create enduring beauty and transform lives.

Optimists pursue goals despite setbacks, confident of success even in the face of adversity.

Connectors have an internal locus of control. They believe that people have control over their fate, so they are very purposeful about their actions. They don't wait for others to make things happen for them, but rather they go through life seeking and seizing opportunities, building track records of achievement that affirm their confidence that they have impact.

Connectors can be agents of change because of their appetite for the new, their ability to articulate a compelling vision, and their confidence that their actions drive results. Others follow their lead because they can envision the well-explained change and the Connector has bolstered them with contagious energy. The Connector's respectful, inclusive, and encouraging behavior mobilizes others to join him/her in driving results and change.

SELF ASSESSMENT

Instructions: Please rate yourself on the following behaviors. A (1) means that this is never true of you, while a (5) means that you always do this.

EXERCISE
Are you Optimistic?

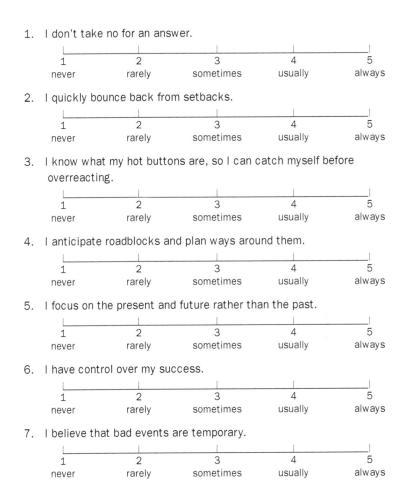

1. I don't take no for an answer.

L_____	_____	_____	_____	
1	2	3	4	5
never	rarely	sometimes	usually	always

2. I quickly bounce back from setbacks.

| 1 | 2 | 3 | 4 | 5 |
| never | rarely | sometimes | usually | always |

3. I know what my hot buttons are, so I can catch myself before overreacting.

| 1 | 2 | 3 | 4 | 5 |
| never | rarely | sometimes | usually | always |

4. I anticipate roadblocks and plan ways around them.

| 1 | 2 | 3 | 4 | 5 |
| never | rarely | sometimes | usually | always |

5. I focus on the present and future rather than the past.

| 1 | 2 | 3 | 4 | 5 |
| never | rarely | sometimes | usually | always |

6. I have control over my success.

| 1 | 2 | 3 | 4 | 5 |
| never | rarely | sometimes | usually | always |

7. I believe that bad events are temporary.

| 1 | 2 | 3 | 4 | 5 |
| never | rarely | sometimes | usually | always |

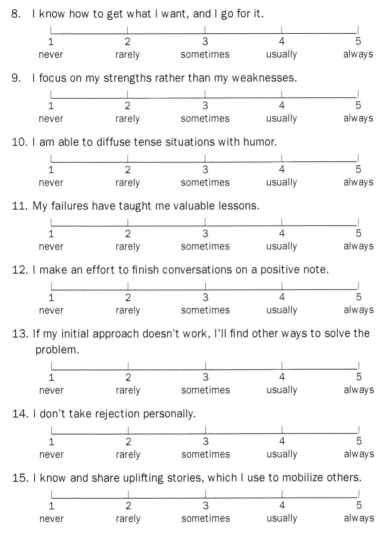

8. I know how to get what I want, and I go for it.

1	2	3	4	5
never	rarely	sometimes	usually	always

9. I focus on my strengths rather than my weaknesses.

1	2	3	4	5
never	rarely	sometimes	usually	always

10. I am able to diffuse tense situations with humor.

1	2	3	4	5
never	rarely	sometimes	usually	always

11. My failures have taught me valuable lessons.

1	2	3	4	5
never	rarely	sometimes	usually	always

12. I make an effort to finish conversations on a positive note.

1	2	3	4	5
never	rarely	sometimes	usually	always

13. If my initial approach doesn't work, I'll find other ways to solve the problem.

1	2	3	4	5
never	rarely	sometimes	usually	always

14. I don't take rejection personally.

1	2	3	4	5
never	rarely	sometimes	usually	always

15. I know and share uplifting stories, which I use to mobilize others.

1	2	3	4	5
never	rarely	sometimes	usually	always

Identify (circle) one behavior to improve in the next year.

Lessons learned from Connectors about Optimism

1. Connectors view displaying optimism as a responsibility to others. Valuing this as a mobilizing force within themselves, they look for opportunities to put a positive yet sincere spin on the topic at hand.

2. Connectors carry uplifting stories in their heads as tools to communicate hope and possibility to others. They find these stories uplifting in their own lives, so they assume others will welcome tales of those who overcame challenges of a similar magnitude.

3. Connectors choose their words carefully, with the intention of ending conversations on a high note. They feel an obligation to be a positive part of another's day. They do this in person or through letters, calls or emails that contain an upbeat twist.

4. When Connectors plan, they anticipate roadblocks and barriers and always have a "Plan B." This approach is used in contingency planning at work and in planning outings with friends and family. They are capable of "turning on a dime" smoothly, confidently bringing others along the new path.

5. Connectors' positive attitudes are not the result of blind faith or unrealistic expectations, but rather from learning in a wide range of settings. They consistently seek solutions, focusing on what works instead of what doesn't, and drawing others into this productive way of thinking. They are positive pragmatists.

6. Connectors are good problem-solvers. They quickly separate key issues from non-essential information and get to the heart of the problem. While they attend to details in solutions, they are not distracted by them in the discernment phase. They know how to break complex challenges into smaller pieces in order to find solutions that work. By including interested parties in the process they increase the likelihood of getting their idea implemented.

7. Connectors do not see themselves as victims. They see a cause and effect relationship between their actions and outcomes and believe that they can and should be able to make things happen. They start transactions expecting to succeed. If they run into obstacles, they find creative ways to overcome or eliminate them. They encourage those around them to operate with their degree of optimism, and look for opportunities to show others that they are making progress toward a goal.

8. Connectors' appetites for variety of all sorts are also expressed in their willingness to accept or initiate change. They see better ways of doing things and are excited by possibilities of what is ahead. They imagine multiple scenarios and articulate the benefits of new projects or conditions to others to help them see alternate scenarios.

9. When Connectors make mistakes or fail in some way, they identify exactly what went wrong. They don't spend much time blaming themselves or others, but rather they learn from their mistakes and move on.

10. Connectors stay focused when things are going wrong. They become vigilant for solutions as they gather facts and call on their network for help. They do not catastrophize but rather hunker down, taking one step at a time in the direction of a solution. They act on their obligation to stay composed in order to be a stabilizing force to those around them.

Behaviors that derail Optimism

1. The inability to use humor to lighten up a conversation and to diffuse tension, allowing the situation to deteriorate or the problem to escalate.

2. Focusing on what is wrong instead of what is right about a person, an idea, a situation, or an opportunity. Being a "wet blanket" or "nay-sayer."

3. Giving up at the first or second sign of trouble. Assuming that barriers are insurmountable and communicating that view to others. Stalling progress and/or checking out because a solution is not immediately visible.

4. Sitting back and waiting for someone else to solve a problem. Assuming either that it's not your responsibility to continue or that you have nothing to contribute to the problem's solution. "Throwing in the towel" early and often.

5. Always relying on the same few people to work with you to solve problems because you don't imagine that "new" people have much to contribute. Acting as if welcoming new people/outsiders to resolve problems is a waste of time. Failing to understand the value of fresh perspectives.

6. Accepting self-sabotaging behaviors brought on by low self-esteem or lack of confidence. Allowing self doubt to rob you of the willingness to try new approaches or to help others to do so.

7. Allowing fear of failure to prevent you from reaching out to people who may not respond positively to you. Denying yourself access to people who are senior to or different from you because you assume that they would not return your call or honor your request.

8. Undermining the efforts of others by focusing on the obstacles and distracting them from continuing to look for solutions.

9. Assuming that someone who is rejecting your idea does not like or respect you. Personalizing criticism and using the criticism as an excuse to stop trying. Generalizing that because you are not doing a specific thing well you are inadequate in some way. Allowing yourself to hide behind the label of victim and settling for less than you believe you have earned. Allowing the ignorance of others to prevent you from making your best contribution.

10. Avoiding situations that you find intimidating; eliminating

discretionary risks by staying inside your small, well-defined comfort zone. Shunning change because of an overwhelming fear of the unknown.

Ten Ways to build Optimism in yourself and others

At work

1. Start paying attention to positive comments people make about you or your work. Make note each time this happens in such a way that you can retrieve the note quickly and easily. Save e-mails that include compliments. Re-read the favorable comments in your performance review. Focus less on what needs improvement and more on what you do well.

2. Read *Now Consider your Strengths* by Marcus Buckingham, and take his advice to heart. Memorize the words that describe your strengths and write them on a card in your wallet. Look at the card when you need a boost.

3. Make a concerted effort to give specific positive feedback to your staff, peers, and customers when they earn it. Send e-mails with your positive thoughts quickly, before you move on to the next obligation. When doing performance reviews, write at least as much in the area about strengths as in the section about developmental needs.

4. Earn a reputation for making others look good. Encourage them by acknowledging their contribution on every occasion. Start meetings by talking about and asking what went well instead of asking about what went wrong. Create a culture of optimism and positive feedback.

At home

5. Follow Oprah Winfrey's lead and start keeping a gratitude journal. Find three reasons to be grateful each day and write them down

before you go to bed, along with one thing that you are looking forward to.

6. Be vigilant about noticing things your children do well. Give them specific positive feedback when they earn it. When they do something wrong or poorly, focus on the deed and talk about how to fix the related problem, rather than labeling your child in a negative way. Frame your constructive criticism by noting, "I love you, but I am not crazy about what you did this time." Preserve their dignity and take your role in developing their optimism seriously.

7. Next time your child breaks a small rule or fails in a small way, ask them to write a very short essay explaining what they did wrong and what action they will take to avoid making the same mistake again. Have them sit down across the table from you and read it. Listen respectfully and add your own suggestions about alternative actions. Instead of nagging or humiliating your child, act like a good coach and help them to be more productive next time.

8. Create a family culture that rewards the effort to try new things. Instead of categorizing and labeling your children, work on giving them "A's for effort" so they become comfortable trying things that don't come easily to them. Choose your language about capabilities carefully, making sure that you are quick to praise a good try. Many parents disguise criticism in the form of teasing, which they mistake as funny. Do not do this or label your child negatively.

In the community

9. Join an organization dedicated to helping children to succeed. Be a mentor or volunteer to tutor a child who needs help with reading. Put yourself in a position to show someone ways to succeed and help them to develop an optimistic attitude.

10. Nominate people for awards who do good things for the community and give others hope. When people ask for nominees,

be someone's advocate and get them recognized. Attend award ceremonies when people are getting recognized for bringing others hope.

"Optimistic people tend to interpret their troubles as transient, controllable, and specific to one situation. Pessimistic people, in contrast, believing that their troubles last forever, undermine everything they do, and are uncontrollable."

Martin Seligman[35]

Results Achiever

"The people who know everyone [Connectors] in some oblique way, may actually run the world.... In a down-to-earth, day-to-day way, they make the world work."

Malcolm Gladwell [36]

MERYL LEVITZ
Greater Philadelphia Tourism Marketing Corporation (GPTMC)

Since its inception in 1996, the Greater Philadelphia Tourism Marketing Corporation (GPTMC) has been a can-do company. Led by Meryl Levitz, GPTMC works hard to build the region's image and make it a booming tourism destination. And booming it is. Over the past 12 years, the  Philadelphia region went from hosting 6.5 million overnight visitors in 1997 (when GPTMC started advertising) to 10.4 million in 2008. The average length of stay is now 2.5 nights, overnight trips have increased more than twice as fast as day trips, and Saturday night has been the busiest night of the week for hotels for over the last five years.

Of the $9.3 billion in economic impact generated by all travelers to Southeast Pennsylvania in 2008, leisure travel to the Philadelphia region generated more than $6 billion. Also in 2008, tourism accounted for 87,000 jobs–that's $2.82 billion in wages–and $1.35 billion in taxes in Philadelphia. Over the past 12 years, growth has been slowed only by the tourism downturn after the tragic events of September 11, 2001, and the economic concerns of 2008.

Adaptability has been key to GPTMC's success. After the events of 9/11, Levitz worked with Philadelphia's hospitality leaders to create a marketing program that would aid the region's short-term recovery. The resulting *Philly's More Fun When You Sleep Over®* campaign has generated 200,000 room nights and $20 million in hotel revenue–and counting. It also helped Philly rebound faster than any city in the U.S.

When GPTMC was challenged again—this time with the global economic crisis—Levitz and her staff created a campaign designed to increase leisure visitation and hotel occupancy, *With Love, Philadelphia XOXO™*. In the changing media landscape, the tourism marketing organization is considered a leader in embracing social media, monitoring developments in the world of print media and adjusting to the different—and increasing—ways people receive messages every day.

Another important part of GPTMC's success is its collaborations with the many great organizations that make up the region's hospitality community. The tourism marketing group works daily with partners in Bucks, Chester, Delaware, Montgomery and Philadelphia counties to make *Philadelphia and The Countryside®* a premier destination through marketing and image building that increases business and promotes the region's vitality.

This coordinated marketing approach helps GPTMC get the word out about Philadelphia through advertising, public relations, cultural tourism programs, gophila.com and uwishunu.com. GPTMC also works closely with local media outlets, transportation providers, and tourist attractions to extend the Philadelphia message to a bigger audience. And they even work with the Philadelphia Police Department to make sure our police officers are informed tourism ambassadors.

Finally, Levitz inspires a passionate staff that keeps GPTMC achieving its desired results. With employees who love this city and region and believe in its potential as a top tourism destination, it's easy to create great work that motivates Philadelphia visits. What's more, GPTMC employees enjoy being tourists in their own town, visiting historic sites, arts and culture attractions, outdoor treasures, sporting events, exhibitions, music venues and everything else that the area offers. Not only does each GPTMC-er love their home, they also share in Levitz's vision for the future of this great region.

Results Achievers have the ability to move ideas forward and stay focused on mutually beneficial outcomes.

Connectors hold themselves and others accountable to deliver as promised. They balance tenacity and persistence in pursuing issues and actions with the perspective of being patient and taking the long view. They measure effectiveness not only by the issues they have impacted but also the breadth, depth, and quality of the relationships formed in the process.

Connectors help others to maintain focus and energy despite obstacles and setbacks. They manage their own relationships and the relationships of others in complex networks to impact outcomes in a positive direction. They view themselves as facilitators of the success of others.

Connectors monitor the efforts of others to ensure that their thoughts and actions are aligned with business or community goals. They set milestones and check interim progress to keep projects on track. They act as champions and advocates, cheering others onward to accomplish tasks, and empowering others to achieve.

SELF ASSESSMENT

Instructions: Please rate yourself on the following behaviors. A (1) means that this is never true of you, while a (5) means that you always do this.

Exercise
Are you a Results Achiever?

1. I hold myself and others accountable to achieve results.

1	2	3	4	5
never	rarely	sometimes	usually	always

2. I make an effort to get and keep everyone on board, working together until the job is done.

1	2	3	4	5
never	rarely	sometimes	usually	always

3. I deliver what I promise efficiently, effectively and on time.

1	2	3	4	5
never	rarely	sometimes	usually	always

4. I have built a diverse network of resources to draw upon to resolve problems.

1	2	3	4	5
never	rarely	sometimes	usually	always

5. I maintain my composure in stressful situations at work and in the community.

1	2	3	4	5
never	rarely	sometimes	usually	always

6. I am vigilant about aligning actions with business priorities and plans.

1	2	3	4	5
never	rarely	sometimes	usually	always

7. I break up the work into smaller segments and set milestones to check progress early and often.

1	2	3	4	5
never	rarely	sometimes	usually	always

8. Others see me as a cheerleader who inspires action.

1	2	3	4	5
never	rarely	sometimes	usually	always

9. I consciously empower others to achieve (versus micro-manage).

1	2	3	4	5
never	rarely	sometimes	usually	always

10. I'm more focused on getting the job done than on getting credit for doing it.

1	2	3	4	5
never	rarely	sometimes	usually	always

11. I make sure that the team understands roles and goals up front.

1	2	3	4	5
never	rarely	sometimes	usually	always

12. I am willing to make a decision with incomplete information.

1	2	3	4	5
never	rarely	sometimes	usually	always

13. I view myself as a facilitator of success for others.

1	2	3	4	5
never	rarely	sometimes	usually	always

14. Challenges fascinate me. I don't give up until I've solved the problem.

1	2	3	4	5
never	rarely	sometimes	usually	always

15. In meetings I focus on bottom-line results and measurable outcomes rather than socializing.

1	2	3	4	5
never	rarely	sometimes	usually	always

Identify (circle) one behavior to improve in the next year.

Lessons learned from Connectors who Achieve Results

1. Connectors are willing to step back and let others lead in order to achieve results. They are more focused on getting the job done than on getting credit for it, and therefore share power, resources, and credit.

2. Connectors are adept at figuring out the steps necessary to get things done. Fascinated by challenges that seem insurmountable to others, they are able to break problems into smaller pieces so that they seem less daunting. Connectors firmly believe they will be able to convince others that with their help, such challenges can be met. They know they can tap the confidence they possess to assemble the skills and find the solutions needed to accomplish the task.

3. Connectors focus on bottom line results and measurable outcomes. While they are adept at orchestrating the process required to get this job done, their satisfaction is linked to achieving goals and completing the task at hand.

4. Connectors communicate their respect for their teammates' competence and commitment. They go out of their way to let each person know that his/her contribution matters. When goals are met, Connectors celebrate formally or informally by thanking each individual for their particular contribution. This behavior not only builds morale, but increases the likelihood that teammates will produce for the Connector next time around.

5. Connectors are quick studies when it comes to problem solving to achieve results. They defer to experts whom they know through networking and keep well informed. They reach out to others who they believe can contribute to the solution even if they don't know them well. The other person responds because of the respectful way the Connector approaches them, and because the Connector's reputation for being enjoyable to work with generally precedes him or her.

6. Connectors hold conversations about expertise in order to learn what others do, and to broaden their own expertise. The cumulative effect of these frequent discussions is that the Connector's own expertise is well known and respected and sought out by others.

7. Connectors are willing and able to deal with ambiguity. They will take on projects even if they don't have the whole picture yet. They enjoy the challenge of an incomplete puzzle and are confident that they can solve it. They see this as challenging rather than risky.

8. Connectors have a well-developed sense of discernment. They can sift through the clutter in a problem faster than most people, who take longer to figure out priorities and correlations. Having been exposed to a range of problems, disciplines, and people, they perceive very few problems as "new." They see through the details to patterns and solutions.

9. Connectors function well under pressure because they have taught themselves to stay calm and composed. They welcome the opportunity to take on responsibility and to organize others to resolve a problem. They get to the heart of the matter quickly, knowing whom to call in their rich social network, and taking one step at a time to handle things efficiently and effectively. They often do this so quietly and quickly behind the scenes that others do not know the Connector's role and contribution, which is just fine with the Connector, who is already off doing other things.

10. Connectors do not rest on their laurels, and are actually rather embarrassed by praise. They are driven to get things done and are not as impressed with accolades as others might be. They are hungry to make a contribution. Being on a team that reaches its goal is exhilarating to the Connector, but as soon as the goal is reached, the Connector is on the alert for the next challenge. They are restless about being fully engaged and can be challenge junkies.

Behaviors that derail the Achievement of Results

1. Lack of following through. Over-promising and under-delivering. Failure to provide the quality of service promised in a timely fashion. Earning a reputation as unreliable.

2. Being insincere about helping someone. Saying that you will meet or mentor them but failing to do so. Talking about what you'll deliver but never getting around to doing it.

3. Wasting time and resources on non-essentials. Focusing efforts on peripheral aspects of a project without getting to the core of it. Socializing for the sake of socializing instead of getting down to business.

4. Failing to achieve buy-in from people who control key resources and outcomes. Ignoring constraints and practical realities in favor of expedient, short-term quick fixes. Allowing things to fall through the cracks and assuming you can take care of them at some undefined later date.

5. Lack of composure in stressful situations. Allowing your emotions and fears to prevent you from doing your best work or pulling your weight with the team. Expressing your anxiety in ways that cause teammates to be anxious. Inability to help keep others calm under pressure and to allay their fears.

6. Inability to make a decision with incomplete information. Waiting too long, missing opportunities to resolve problems before they escalate or the situation deteriorates.

7. Acting unpredictably and unreliably when others are counting on you to stay strong and stable. Waffling on decisions, slowing down the process and eroding others' confidence in your leadership.

8. Producing inconsistent results, confusing others about your skills and reliability. Failure to produce strong results across a variety of situations. Having a narrow definition of your potential contribution.

9. Jumping into action to solve a problem before you have taken the time to bring the rest of the team on board. Failure to define the goals and roles before you are clear on the scope and nature of the work.

10. Focusing on power positions and what's in it for you to be involved in an initiative rather than considering the good of the whole and the need for action and results.

Ten ways to Achieve Results

At work

1. Clarify goals and roles up front in projects and in meetings. Make sure each person knows why they are there, and that the scope of their assignments does not overlap.

2. Create a planning document that includes milestones, deadlines, and accountabilities. Offer to do this, even if you are not running the project, in order to ensure that there is sufficient structure, follow through, and discipline to get the job done.

3. Earn a reputation for making deadlines, delivering what you promise and being willing to go the extra mile to get things done.

4. Give credit to members of your team, praising them specifically in public and in private, verbally, and in writing.

At home

5. Build credibility by showing up on time for obligations at home. Treat your personal calendar with the same discipline you use with your schedule at work. Do not cancel outings. Make things happen for your family the way you do for your colleagues and customers.

6. Teach your children how to keep their schedule. Give them

calendars and show them how to use them. Reward them in small ways for being organized and for being on time.

7. Create a family culture of achievement by encouraging everyone to set goals. Celebrate their achievements and talk about what each person is doing well.

In the community

8. Take minutes for the community meetings you are involved in. Make note of specific follow-up actions and deadlines, as well as who has volunteered for what. Circulate minutes to everyone with follow-up responsibilities shortly after the meeting.

9. Offer to chair the board of an organization that you care about deeply. Lead the board through a strategic planning process to get agreement on goals and expectations. Rally the board to implement the plan.

10. Instead of complaining about community issues to friends and family, step up and volunteer to do something. Call your neighbors together, join a committee, or get active in politics. Just do it!

"It is not enough to be compassionate; you must act."

Dalai Lama

Self-Starter

"Throw yourself into life as someone who makes a difference, accepting that you may not understand how and why."

Benjamin Zander [37]

HUGH LONG

Regional President, Community Banking, Wachovia

Hugh Long came to Philadelphia in 2003 to lead the Pennsylvania/ Delaware region for Wachovia Bank. Having been through a number of mergers, he noticed that while many bankers had an affinity for internal focus, he viewed his job as public.

"People want to know someone at the bank. There is no better way to make a difference in the community than by allowing people to get to know you."

His guiding principle is, "Business goes where it is invited and stays where it is well taken care of." His outside-orientation enabled Long to make a name for himself far more quickly than most other CEO's who are new to town. While the average Connector has been in town 24 years, Long made the list with just three years of tenure.

Long was invited to join many organizations as a new CEO in town. His knack for matching his experience and skills with the best opportunity to have an impact in the community quickly led him to choose the Greater Philadelphia Chamber of Commerce's budding regional economic development effort as his signature civic effort.

Using his experience with similar initiatives in Atlanta and Washington, D.C., Long became the champion of the Chamber's newly minted Select Greater Philadelphia marketing organization. He cemented his leadership by becoming the first executive to pledge $1 million to Select. "We found a way to become more important to the Chamber and help advance an agenda that was valuable to them and the region. Our support of regional economic development provided a platform for greater visibility and more opportunities."

Long burst on the scene with a refreshing degree of optimism and a bias toward action. He focused on "changing the dialogue of what is possible in Philadelphia and doing it in a public way." He's a big believer in coalition building and inclusion. Perhaps that is why, six years after he first arrived in this city—despite the tumult in the market in the industry—he's still thriving and in charge.

Connectors have a natural bias toward action.

Connectors offer their expertise or support without any expectation of getting anything in return. They believe that their actions will eventually lead to a useful outcome. They offer suggestions on how to improve things at work and at home. Connectors initiate actions that lead to connections among others. They plan ahead and actively invite others into the planning process.

Connectors anticipate situations well in advance and act to avoid problems that are not obvious to others. They try new and creative solutions, using judgment to minimize risk. They search for new ideas and trends, which may lead to entrepreneurial opportunities. They scan the local environment for opportunities to be useful, and reach out to others to make improvements or move them toward a specific agenda.

SELF ASSESSMENT

Instructions: Please rate yourself on the following behaviors. A (1) means that this is never true of you, while a (5) means that you always do this.

EXERCISE
Are you a Self-Starter?

1. I offer my expertise and support, expecting nothing in return.

1	2	3	4	5
never	rarely	sometimes	usually	always

2. I make suggestions on how to improve things at work and at home.

1	2	3	4	5
never	rarely	sometimes	usually	always

3. I reach out to people whom I find interesting.

1	2	3	4	5
never	rarely	sometimes	usually	always

4. I plan ahead and include others in the process.

1	2	3	4	5
never	rarely	sometimes	usually	always

5. I act quickly in time of crisis, calling upon my network for help if necessary.

1	2	3	4	5
never	rarely	sometimes	usually	always

6. I can spot future problems and opportunities before others do.

1	2	3	4	5
never	rarely	sometimes	usually	always

7. I'm willing to try creative solutions.

1	2	3	4	5
never	rarely	sometimes	usually	always

8. People refer to me as entrepreneurial and innovative.

1	2	3	4	5
never	rarely	sometimes	usually	always

9. I take an active interest in trends and new ideas.

1	2	3	4	5
never	rarely	sometimes	usually	always

10. I assemble people to move an agenda forward at work and in the community.

1	2	3	4	5
never	rarely	sometimes	usually	always

11. I take time to send notes expressing appreciation to people who accomplish something that inspires me.

1	2	3	4	5
never	rarely	sometimes	usually	always

12. I assume that if I reach out to someone they will respond favorably.

1	2	3	4	5
never	rarely	sometimes	usually	always

13. I am bold about raising my hand to help or volunteer.

1	2	3	4	5
never	rarely	sometimes	usually	always

14. I do my homework and research people and situations before approaching them.

1	2	3	4	5
never	rarely	sometimes	usually	always

15. I'm more likely to make an error of commission than an error of omission.

1	2	3	4	5
never	rarely	sometimes	usually	always

Identify (circle) one behavior to improve in the next year.

Lessons learned about Self-Starting

1. Connectors are capable of inspiring themselves and others into action. They are energetic by nature and do not sit back and wait to be asked. They are easily engaged when an exciting yet practical new approach is presented to them, and they like to get involved.

2. Connectors are rarely at a loss for words. Whether extraverted or introverted, they will step up and start asking people about themselves and what they are working on. They find these exchanges energizing.

3. Connectors reach out to check in with friends or acquaintances periodically as an end in and of itself. They will jot notes, phone or call for lunch simply to stay in touch.

4. Connectors step in to move processes forward even in the absence of extensive planning or complete information. They push for progress and remind others about the need to meet goals.

5. Connectors are unlikely to claim that they are too busy to get involved. No matter how much responsibility they are juggling at a given time, they will drop everything (carefully) or set things aside to help a person or project in need. They seem to seize more opportunities than other people, and they thrive on being overextended.

6. Connectors push for opportunities for people to get to know each other. They host events, meetings, and parties, and they take time to get people to talk to each other.

7. Connectors may insinuate themselves into situations where others like them may assume that they are not welcome. They are confident that their contribution is valuable and that they can move the process forward. Their strong interpersonal skills enable them to join new groups easily and to adapt well.

8. Connectors like being where the action is. They are energized

by crowds and enthusiastic about causes. They seek situations in which they are part of a group of active change agents who are willing to work with the Connector to spread the word about an exciting new initiative.

9. Connectors volunteer for new projects, committees, and boards. They want to be on teams that make things happen. They want to work with other bright people to bring about change in the workplace or community. They will volunteer to help without fanfare or expectation of payback.

10. Connectors write to the newspaper and to elected officials. They have strong reactions to issues related to the common good and believe it is their duty and right to speak up. Their diplomatic skills and organized thinking make them good at this.

Behaviors that derail Self-Starting

1. Procrastinating and waiting to be asked instead of jumping up and volunteering to serve. Hiding behind your workload at work or at home, claiming to be too busy to add one more thing to your agenda.

2. Only volunteering to help when the payback is obvious. Letting everyone know that if you do something for them you expect to be repaid quickly and well. Keeping score about these things and withholding help to people who have not done enough for you.

3. Being a perfectionist and limiting yourself to activities in which you have expertise and experience. Failing to try new things because you might not do them well.

4. Failure to prioritize tasks at work and at home so that you take on too many obligations and don't know what to handle first and what can wait. Your discomfort around these obligations can paralyze you as you realize you are so over-committed that you are not doing anything particularly well.

5. Being unwilling to make a move without checking with your boss first. Granted, some issues require checking, but if you feel that need to check every step of the way, you are in over your head and are not developing your own skills sufficiently.

6. Jumping into a new group or project without doing your homework first. Failing to identify the key decision-makers and the organization's or program's priorities.

7. Moving so fast that others cannot catch up. You may find that you have figured out how to solve a problem before others even know what that problem is. If you put yourself too far ahead of the team and fail to bring them up to speed, they will become demoralized and may stop trying.

8. Labeling yourself as shy and always staying in the background of conversations. Preferring to be a bystander watching in the wings instead of a player on the court. Hiding behind shyness is a choice that limits your options.

9. Failure to reach out to help younger people by mentoring, advising, or simply listening to them. Believing that you would not enjoy mentoring and that you have very little to offer a mentee. This sort of small thinking closes doors instead of opening them.

10. Skipping meetings, events, celebrations and appointments. Mismanaging your calendar so that dates are missing or wrong. Disappointing people who were hoping to celebrate with you or to thank you for your role in their development.

Ten Ways to Self-Start

At work

1. Get correspondence cards imprinted with your name. Mark your calendar to send at least one per week to a peer, staff member, or client who does something well or is celebrating

an accomplishment. Say something specific and upbeat. Say something favorable about them to their boss.

2. Volunteer for a new project or a community board or team.

3. If you feel strongly about a project or initiative, volunteer to get involved. Don't wait to be asked.

4. Reinforce staff members who volunteer and show initiative. Praise them in public and in private. Let it be known that initiative will be recognized and rewarded.

At home

5. Offer to plan a family trip to a site where you can learn something and have fun at the same time. Make arrangements carefully. Orchestrate the trip so logistics are transparent. Do the homework and the planning to create a great experience for the others.

6. Reward your children for showing initiative. Talk about people volunteering and stepping up to a challenge. Let them know that showing initiative is a family value.

7. Step up to do something that you have been putting off at home. Run errands before you are asked. Look around the house for opportunities to exceed your spouse's expectations by fixing something without being asked.

8. Discourage procrastination on the part of your children. Show them how to plan projects and schedule things to avoid the last minute rush. Give them calendars and planners early on so that they develop the habit of being proactive instead of reactive.

In the community

9. Read the editorial page and respond with your opinion. If you like a story, write to the journalist and express your appreciation.

10. Form a team to address a community issue that people have been complaining about. Take responsibility for hosting the meeting and inviting people who have a local concern. Welcome and introduce people, take notes, and keep the process moving ahead until the problem is solved.

"We cannot live only for ourselves. A thousand fibers connect us with our fellow man; and along these fibers, as sympathetic threads, our actions run as causes, and they come back as effects."

Herman Melville

Connector Competency
Action Plan

Instructions: Look at the results of your self assessment for each connector competency. List the encircled behavior on the lines below:

C ommunity Catalyst: _____

O ther-Oriented: _____

N etwork Hubs: _____

N avigating Mazes: _____

E mpowering Passion: _____

C urious: _____

T rustworthy: _____

O ptimistic: _____

R esults Achievers: _____

S elf Starters: _____

1. What 3 areas will you work on improving this year?

   _____

   _____

   _____

2. The following person does these things well:

   _____

3. I will connect with this role model to ask his/her advice by: [month/date]

   _____

4. What three specific things will improve as a result of my efforts to improve my Connector skills?

   A. _____

   B. _____

   C. _____

Part III

Afterword

A Social Imperative

by Karen Stephenson, Ph.D.

Connecting In Philadelphia

If you grow up in this country or become a naturalized citizen,
sooner or later you read about the democratic experiment
conducted in Philadelphia in 1776 that led to the formation of the
United States of America. But how many of us know about another
social experiment conducted in that same city 230 years later, by Liz
Dow and the nonprofit organization LEADERSHIP Philadelphia?
That's what this book is about.

LEADERSHIP Philadelphia defines its mission thus: "to
mobilize and connect the talent of the private sector to serve the
community." In 2005, with the help of print media, television, radio,
and the Internet, Liz Dow, president of the nonprofit, and a core
team of nine other volunteers embarked on a journey and launched
a process whereby citizens could identify "unsung heroes" soldiering
acts of public good. Here was everyone's opportunity to recognize
extraordinary Philadelphians for their great works and shine a light on
civic engagement.

It was a noble endeavor, for amid the cacophony of public
scandals and financial meltdowns, the scorched earth of the human
heart was laid bare—weary, cynical, disinclined and disengaged.
Despite disillusionment—or perhaps because of it—people took time

out to nominate the ordinary citizen doing extraordinary things. This uncanny ability to altruistically recognize others is an evolutionary social imperative. Millennia ago, that same ability enabled our primordial ancestors to cooperate and overcome overwhelming environmental odds. So what is this alchemy of the human heart? The answer is TRUST.

And we believe Trust to be an essential element in meeting the challenges of Philadelphia in the 21st century as it was for our ancestors millennia ago. We may not face the same challenges Benjamin Franklin faced 230 years ago, but we still need to embrace our huddled masses to solve complex problems that no single individual or group can solve alone.

Considering Connection

F inding connectors raises important issues for 21st century leadership and what it means to build sustainable trusted networks in connected collaborative communities. Never before in human history have we ever been so inter-connected. This has important implications for how we conceive of connection, and secondarily, how we use social media or technology to become connected.

For example, most people think of connection as a trusted relationship between two individuals, not a force field binding a village, a culture, a community, or a country together. Trust between two individuals is difficult enough, but trust is truly tested when it is stretched over three or more individuals. Friends of friends is an expression of how trust can be stretched from a two-person relationship to a three or more person "multiple relationship." These multiple relationships are significant, because at least two individuals are *indirectly* connected through a common third party.

In the real world, we wade through thousands of indirect relationships every day and are mostly oblivious to them. Yet these indirect exchanges[1] can affect who we meet, how we make decisions, and often what we say. The popular phrase "six degrees of separation" tries to capture this point; however, it also misses an important point. Its significance lies not in how many degrees of separation actually exist, but in our "position" in a network of indirect linkages. Human beings cannot see indirect linkages, so our ignorance of where we fit in a larger picture impacts how we get connected to others, or don't.

A different example of connection is that no matter how sophisticated social media has become, it cannot advance beyond or trump trust. You can have the most cutting edge technology at the fingertips of a team, but if the members of the team don't trust one another, nothing—*or worse*—will result. Sub-optimal technology, on the other hand, can be overcome when a trusted team tackles a problem, precisely because collaboration flows at the speed of trust, not bandwidth.

So the lesson here is that connection can be both capricious and calculating, but it certainly is not random; it exists only where there is either trust or technology, and preferably both operating together and not at the expense of each other.

---

[1]Levi-Strauss, the famous anthropologist, classified several types of exchanges and called this version "generalized exchange" (see *The Elementary Structures of Kinship*, 1969).

Connecting Connectors

While one cannot legislate the formation of trust, one can certainly provide opportunities for trust to grow and bring together connectors once they are identified. Think about it. Imagine a world where sharing resources among these super connectors at this supra-level might connect neighborhoods better than any form of government-mandated policy. Imagine that long-stalled civic projects and public works might get a boost from these civic super stars. Once connectors are identified, the next logical step is to convene them so they can meet one another. Here is where social chemistry takes off and is at its most robust turning into a golden trust. Trust is the central rationale of the Philadelphia connector study. All of us are part of great experiments in our own communities, and we are also part of the problem. But if we can reach across our differences to trust one another, we can become the solution.

Never doubt that a small group of thoughtful, committed citizens can change the world. Indeed, it is the only thing that ever has.

Margaret Mead, 1935

Author's Note

If one were to identify the most powerful competency shared by Connectors in the current millennium, it would likely be Optimism. In an environment over-run with public scandal, corporate greed, unethical politicians, and the rapid decline of common civility, it would be easy for everyone to just throw up their hands and crawl into a cave. However, the abiding optimism of Connectors enables them to move above and beyond the darker pockets of human behavior and forge ahead in their missions.

In the home, Connecting has always been the linchpin that holds the family together and keeps its members strong enough to support each other–and to venture forth into the world. Without mutual cooperation inside the family, without parents setting examples for appreciating, nurturing and celebrating the community, the world outside would be chaos.

In business and in the community at large, we can see Connector collaborations paralleling those of technology–and vice-versa. Connectors, in fact, are themselves a metaphor for the way information now travels across electronic/digital networks. Viral emails, for example, are the offspring of Connectors taken to the nth power! Or are they? Perhaps we're facing a chicken-and-egg scenario. . . . Do social networks exist because of Connectors? Or do Connectors thrive because of the existence of social networks? Does the answer matter? Probably not. The Connectors and their connections are the point.

Home is where Connectors are born. Business is where Connectors serve to keep the cogs of commerce moving. And the community is where home and business meet in a glorious convergence of common purpose and common benefit–all thanks to the human phenomenon known as the Connector.

You can be a Connector. In fact, if you have done the exercises in this book, you already are on your way to being a Connector. Now it's up to you to take the characteristics you recognize within yourself and use them for the greater good–at home, at work, and in your community.

Liz Dow, President
LEADERSHIP Philadelphia

Methodology

Connectors were found through a methodology based upon Netform CEO Karen Stephenson's work and altered to conduct this innovative project. This consisted of the following steps.

1. Identify a multi-disciplinary team to shape the scope and nature of the project. Project leaders should have standing in the community and a reputation and platform that demonstrate credibility when working with leaders across sectors.

2. Hold focus groups with key community leaders to introduce the concept and process and to get local feedback.

3. Send a viral email request that citizens identify Connectors by sharing specific names in response to the following seven questions:

> Imagine that every five years, a research organization called the "World's Great Places" publishes a list of the most wonderful places in the world. The head of the World's Great Places tells you that the greater Philadelphia region has been evaluated and is on the short list of metropolitan areas with the most potential to be the "Greatest Place" for 2012. You are asked to form a team of the most talented people whom you personally know in the greater Philadelphia area. These people will help you think about what the area can do between now and the time the contest ends—in 2012—that will ensure that Philadelphia wins the award of the greatest place in the world.

> a. Who do you consider to be particularly innovative; who could bring "big picture" ideas to this effort?
> b. Who do you think has the expertise or expert knowledge to turn great ideas into reality?

    c. Whom do you know who has the integrity, concern for the common good, and guts to help get this done?

    d. Who do you consider to be an effective implementer? Who would roll up his or her sleeves and see this work through with you to the end?

    e. Whom could you depend on to help bring together and wisely coordinate the area's resources to meet this challenge?

    f. Whom in your own neighborhood or local community could you depend on to help make your neighborhood or community the best in the world?

    g. Imagine that you need advice about an important issue. Whom outside of your own race, class, social circle, gender, religion, age group, etc., would you consult?

4. Enlist the help of local newspapers, blogs, and other hub organizations to solicit responses.

5. Count responses to determine most frequently listed individuals/Connectors.

6. Research names submitted to find contact information (and to clarify which "John Smith").

7. Contact top 100 to ask permission to publish their names in related articles.

8. Announce Connector names and cover stories of their accomplishments and contributions.

9. Convene Connectors to honor and identify opportunities to collaborate.

10. Encourage/invite Connectors to assist with community projects.

Appendix B
Connectors

The following professionals were identified as Connectors by citizens of Philadelphia in 2006.

Experienced Connectors

Dean Adler	Lubert-Adler Real Estate Funds
Peggy Amsterdam	Greater Philadelphia Cultural Alliance
Bruce Aronow	Managers Investment Group
Sheila Ballen	Pennsylvania Department of Education
Wendy Beetlestone	Hangley Aronchick Segal & Pudlin
Richard A. Bendis	Bendis Investment Group LLC
Chuck Bragitikos	Vibrant Development Group LLC
Karen D. Buchholz	Comcast Communications
Duane Bumb	Philadelphia Department of Commerce
Della Clark	The Enterprise Center
John Claypool	AIA Philadelphia
Louis Coffey	Wolf, Block, Schorr & Solis-Cohen LLP
Richard J. Cohen	Philadelphia Health Management Corporation
David L. Cohen	Comcast Corporation
Patricia A. Coulter	Urban League of Philadelphia, Inc.
Helen Cunningham	Samuel S. Fels Fund
Nick DeBenedictis	Aqua America, Inc.
Kevin Dow	Wachovia Bank
Liz Dow	LEADERSHIP Philadelphia
Nancy Dunleavy	Dunleavy and Associates
Joseph A. Dworetzky	Hangley Aronchick Segal & Pudlin
Dwight Evans	PA House of Representatives
David R. Fair	United Way of Southeastern Pennsylvania
Varsovia Fernandez	Greater Philadelphia Hispanic Chamber of Commerce
Graham Finney	The Conservation Company (TCC)
Stephanie Gambone	The Philadelphia Youth Network
Daniel Garofalo	University of Pennsylvania

Valerie V. Gay	Temple University
Teresa Gillen	City of Philadelphia
Eva Gladstein	Philadelphia Empowerment Zone
Jane Golden	Philadelphia Mural Arts Program
Nancy A. Goldenberg	Center City District
Dolph W. Goldenburg	William Way LGBT Community Center
Phil Goldsmith	GoldsmithKahnAssociates
Stephen M. Goodman	Morgan Lewis & Bockius, LLP
Rosemarie B. Greco	Commonwealth of Pennsylvania
Derek Green	Office of Councilwoman Marian Tasco
Alan Greenberger	MGA Partners
Melissa Grimm	Gramercy Group, LLC
Alison Grove	Alison Grove and Associates
Gloria Guard	People's Emergency Center
Craig Hamilton	The Philadelphia Orchestra
William P. Hankowsky	Liberty Property Trust
Irene Hannan	Citizens Bank
Jonathan G. Herrmann	Campus Philly
Lissa Hilsee	Philadelphia Cares
Kenny Holdsman	Academy for Educational Development
Steve Honeyman	Eastern Philadelphia Organizing Project
Feather Houstoun	William Penn Foundation
Mark A. Hughes	City of Philadelphia
Farah J. Jimenez	Mt. Airy, USA
Ernest E. Jones	Philadelphia Workforce Development
Loree D. Jones	City of Philadelphia
Sam Katz	Leverage Partners LLC
Joshua Kopelman	First Round Capital
Meryl Levitz	Greater Philadelphia Tourism Marketing
Paul R. Levy	Center City District
Charisse Lillie	Comcast Cable Corporation
Hugh C. Long	Wachovia
Brett H. Mandel	Philadelphia FORWARD
William J. Marrazzo	WHYY
Alba Martinez	Vanguard
Sharmain Matlock Turner	Greater Philadelphia Urban Affairs Coalition
Stephen P. Mullin	Econsult Corporation
Stephanie Naidoff	City of Philadelphia, Department of Commerce
James Nevels	The Swarthmore Group

Jeremy Nowak	The Reinvestment Fund
Michael Nutter	City of Philadelphia
Marlene L. Olshan	Big Brothers Big Sisters Southeastern PA
Cherelle Parker	Pennsylvania House of Representatives
Marsha Perelman	Woodforde Energy
Charles Pizzi	Tasty Baking Company
Pedro A. Ramos	Blank Rome LLP
Edward G. Rendell	Commonwealth of Pennsylvania
Estelle Richman	Commonwealth of Pennsylvania
Rebecca Rimel	The Pew Foundation
Howard Ross	LLR Partners
Ronald Rubin	Pennsylvania Real Estate Investment Trust
Christopher Satullo	WHYY
Edward Schwartz	Institute for the Study of Civic Values in Philadelphia
Mary Scullion	Project HOME
Josh Sevin	City of Philadelphia
Laura Shubilla	Philadelphia Youth Network
Zachery Stalberg	The Committee of Seventy
Patrick M. Starr	PA Environmental Council
Harris M. Steinberg	University of Pennsylvania, School of Design
Marc Stier	Intellectual Heritage Program at Temple University
Rob Stuart	Evolve Strategies
E.Mitchell Swann	MDC Systems
David B. Thornburgh	Fels Institute of Government
Ellen Toplin	StarToplin
Nicholas Torres	Congreso de Latinos Unidos
Joe Torsella	National Constitution Center
Andrew Toy	Campaign for Andy Toy 07
Paul Vallas	School District of Philadelphia
Robert Weber	Antiphony Partners, LLC
Melissa Weiler Gerber	WOMEN'S WAY
Ken Weinstein	Trolley Car Diner & Ice Cream Shoppe
Judith A. Wicks	White Dog Community Enterprises
D-L Wormley	NeighborhoodsNow
Lynn H. Yeakel	Drexel University College of Medicine

The following professionals were identified as emerging Connectors by citizens of Philadelphia in 2008.

Emerging Connectors

Pauline M. Abernathy	City of Philadelphia
Brian Abernathy	City Council–Office of Frank DiCicco
Erica Atwood	City of Philadelphia
Chelsea Badeau	Comcast Cable Corporation
Brad Baldia	South East Philadelphia Collaborative
Matthew Bergheiser	University City District, Philadelphia
Mitchell Bormack	TRC Companies, Inc.
Jamahal Boyd	JB Productions
Chanel Broadus	Community College of Philadelphia
Steve Burda	SunGard Data Systems
Vanja Buvac	The Cadence Watch Company
Kevin Cafferky	Philadelphia Opportunities Industrialization Center, Inc.
Dawn Chavous	Office of Senator Anthony H. Williams
Aaron J. Cohen	Arena Strategies
Danielle Cohn	Philadelphia Convention & Visitors Bureau
Harry Cook	Philly1.com, InfoVoter Technologies, Double Chai
Eric Cushing	Special Olympics Pennsylvania
Melissa DeShields	Community Development Associates, Inc.
Deborah Diamond	Greater Philadelphia Tourism Marketing Corp.
Anthony DiMeo III	RENAMITY Public Relations & Special Events
Amit Dogra	BNY Mellon
Jamie Elfant	Franklin's Paine Skatepark Fund
Cynthia Figueroa	Women Against Abuse
David Forde	Office of Councilwoman Blondell Reynolds Brown
Jocelyn Gabrynowicz Hill	McCarter & English, LLP
Stephanie Gambone	The Philadelphia Youth Network
Tatiana Garcia-Granados	East Park Revitalization Alliance
Jack Garfinkle	Pepper Hamilton LLP
Shira Goodman	Pennsylvanians for Modern Courts
Steve Grandizio	Friendly Mortgage

Derek Green	Office of Councilwoman Marian Tasco
Kevin Greenberg	Flaster/Greenberg P.C.
Claire M. Greenwood	Select Greater Philadelphia
Melissa Grimm	Gramercy Group, LLC
Helen Gym	Asian Americans United
Elinor Haider	City of Philadelphia-Office of the Deputy Mayor
Kirsty Halliday	SCA Americas
Tine Hansen-Turton	Philadelphia Health Management Corporation
Matty Hart	Solutions for Progress
Julie Hawkins	Greater Philadelphia Cultural Alliance
John Hawkins	S.R. Wojdak & Associates
Greg Heller	Delaware Valley Regional Planning Commission
Bob Henon	Electricians IBEW Local 98
Jonathan G. Herrmann	Campus Philly
Sheila M. Hess	Independence Blue Cross
Julia Hinckley	PA Department of Public Welfare
Lauren Hirshon	Philadelphia Workforce Investment Board
Lauren Holland	Institute for Women's Health and Leadership
Kate Houstoun	Ready, Willing & Able
Blake Jennelle	AntHillz.com
Loree D. Jones	City Year Greater Philadelphia
Christine Knapp	Citizens for Pennsylvania's Future (PennFuture)
Emily Landsburg	BlackGold Biofuels
Austin Lavin	WorkNOLA.com
Ken Lawrence	Temple University
Kelly Lee	Innovation Philadelphia
Yael Lehmann	The Food Trust
Paul Lima	Lima Consulting
Anne Mahlum	Back On My Feet
Brett H. Mandel	Philadelphia FORWARD
Gabriel Mandujano	The Enterprise Center
Brett Mapp	Old City District
Ayanna K. Matlock	JRH Electronics, LLC
Matt McClure	Ballard Spahr Andrews & Ingersoll
Elizabeth Miller	Community Design Collaborative
Sirena Moore	Elohim Cleaning Contractors
Ted Mucellin	City of Philadelphia
Jessica Natali	US Department of Justice
Alisa Orduna-Sneed	People's Emergency Center

Cherelle Parker	Pennsylvania House of Representatives
Danyl S. Patterson	The Patterson Law Firm
Bret Perkins	Comcast Cable Communications, Inc.
Cicely Peterson-Mangum	Logan CDC
A. Grant Phelan	Klehr, Harrison, Harvey, Branzburg & Ellers
Arun Prabhakaran	Solutions for Progress
Sulaiman Rahman	urbanphilly.com
Ajay Raju	Reed Smith LLP
Gina Renzi	The Rotunda
Jenn Rezeli	Re: Vision Architecture
Angelina Riley	PA Department of Health
Pedro J. Rivera	Wachovia Wealth Management
David C. Ryan	PricewaterhouseCoopers LLP
Bradford Sandler	Benesch, Friedlander, Coplan & Aronoff LLP
Barbara Saverino	Greater Philadelphia Chamber of Commerce
Josh Sevin	City of Philadelphia
Jan S. Shaeffer	St. Christopher's Foundation for Children
Seth Shapiro	The Nauset Group
Christopher Sheridan	Committee of Seventy
Sonya Springer	SunGard Availability Services
Nicholas Torres	Congreso de Latinos Unidos
Erin Trent	Sneaker Villa
Sozi Tulante	Hangley Aronchick Segal & Pudlin
Kristen Vieira Traynor	PricewaterhouseCoopers LLP
Ronald Walker	Bethany Baptist Church
Mailee Walker	Claneil Foundation
Melissa Weiler Gerber	WOMEN'S WAY
Laura I. Weinbaum	Project H.O.M.E.
Leigh Whitaker	SugarHouse Casino
Sara Woods	Philadelphia VIP
Rachel Zimmerman	InLiquid

Endnotes

Part I

1 Malcolm Gladwell, "Six Degrees of Lois Weisberg," *The New Yorker,* 11 Jan., 1999, p. 63.
2. Gladwell, "Six Degrees," p. 63.
3. Malcolm Gladwell, *The Tipping Point,* New York: Little, Brown and Company, 2000, p. 38.
4. Gladwell, *The Tipping Point,* p. 43-45.
5. Roger Horchow, Sally Horchow, *The Art of Friendship,* New York: A Quirk Packaging Book, 2005, p. 7.
6. Gladwell, "Six Degrees," p. 60.
7. Wayne Baker, *Achieving Success Through Social Capital,* New York: John Wiley and Sons, 2000, pp. 1-2.
8. Jonathan Berry, Ed Keller, *The Influentials,* New York: The Free Press, 2003.
9. Gladwell, *The Tipping Point,* 264.
10. *The Tipping Point,* p. 275.
11. *The Tipping Point,* p. 280.
12. Walter Isaacson, *Benjamin Franklin,* New York: Simon and Schuster, 2003, p. 55.
13. Isaacson, p. 102.
14. Isaacson, p. 493.
15. Isaacson, p. 102.
16. Isaacson, p. 55.
17. Isaacson, p. 56.
18. Isaacson, p. 493.
19. Isaacson, p. 493.

Part II

20. Berry, Keller, p. 100.
21. Stephen R. Covey, *The Seven Habits of Highly Effective People,* New York: Fireside, 1989, p. 13.
22. Berry, Keller, p. 31.
23. Covey, p. 219.

24. Covey, p. 207.
25. Berry, Keller, p. 14.
26. Gladwell, "Six Degrees"
27. Gladwell, "Six Degrees."
28. Rosamund Zander, Benjamin Zander, *The Art of Possibility,* New York: Simon and Schuster, 2003, p. 125.
29. Robert L. Cross, Andrew Parker, *The Hidden Power of Social Networks,* Boston, MA: Harvard Business School Publishing Corporation, 2004, p. 57.
30. Ross Bernstein, *Remembering Herbie,* New Brighton, MN: Printing Enterprises, 2003, p. 85.
31. Cross, Parker, p. 59.
32. Douglas B. Richardson, *Networking,* New York: John Wiley and Sons, 1994, p.193.
33. Bernstein, p. 76.
34. Zander, Zander, p. 163.
35. Martin Seligman, Ph.D, Karen Reivich, MA, Lisa Jaycox, Ph.D, and Jane Gilham, Ph.D, *The Optimistic Child,* New York: Harper Collins, 2002, p. 10.
36. Gladwell, "Six Degrees."
37. Zander, Zander, p. 58.

Bibliography

Barbara Arneil, *Diverse Communities,* New York: Cambridge University Press, 2006.

Wayne Baker, *Achieving Success Through Social Capital,* New York: John Wiley and Sons, 2000.

Albert-László Barabási, *Linked,* New York: PLUME, Penguin Group, 2002 and 2003.

John Bartlett, *Bartlett's Familiar Quotations,* Boston: Little, Brown and Company, 17th Edition, 2002.

Ross Bernstein, *Remembering Herbie,* New Brighton, MN: Printing Enterprises, 2003.

Jonathan Berry, Ed Keller, *The Influentials,* New York: The Free Press, 2003.

Betty Lou Bettner, Ph.D., Amy Lew, Ph.D., *Raising Kids Who Can,* New York: Harper Collins, 1992.

David Bornstein, *How to Change the World,* New York: Oxford University Press, 2004.

Bill Bradley, *The New American Story,* New York: Random House, 2007.

Ronald S. Burt, *Brokerage and Closure,* New York: Oxford University Press, 2005.

Frank Capra, *It's A Wonderful Life,* Los Angeles, CA: Republic Pictures, 1947.

Stephen R. Covey, *The Seven Habits of Highly Effective People,* New York: Fireside, 1989.

Stephen R. Covey with Rebecca R. Merrill, *The Speed of Trust,* New York: Free Press, A Division of Simon and Schuster, 2006.

Robert L. Cross, Andrew Parker, *The Hidden Power of Social Networks,* Boston, MA: Harvard Business School Publishing Corporation, 2004.

Edited by Richardson Dilworth, *Social Capital in the City,* Philadelphia: Temple University Press, 2006.

Basil Entwistle, *Making Cities Work,* Pasadena, CA: Hope Publishing House, 1992.

Keith Ferrazzi with Tahl Raz, *Never Eat Alone,* New York: Broadway Business, 2005.

Thomas Friedman, *The World is Flat,* Farrar, Straus, and Giroux, 2005.

John W. Gardner, *On Leadership,* New York: The Free Press, A Division of Simon and Schuster, Inc., 1990.

Jeffrey Gitomer, *Little Book of Connections,* Austin, TX: Bard Press, 2006.

Malcolm Gladwell, "Six Degrees of Lois Weisberg," New York: *The New Yorker,* pages 52-63, January 11, 1999.

Malcolm Gladwell, *The Tipping Point,* New York: Little, Brown and Company, 2000.

Daniel Goleman, *Social Intelligence,* New York: Bantam Book, a Division of Random House, Inc., 2006.

Edward Hallowell, *The Childhood Roots of Adult Happiness,* New York: The Random House Publishing Group, 2002.

David Halpern, *Social Capital,* Cambridge CB2 1 UR, UK: Polity Press, 2005.

Sonya Hamlin, *How To Talk So People Listen,* New York: Harper Collins, 2006.

Steve Harrison, *The Manager's Book of Decencies,* New York: McGraw-Hill, 2007.

Chip Heath, Dan Heath, *Made to Stick,* New York: Random House, 2007.

Roger Horchow, Sally Horchow, *The Art of Friendship,* New York: A Quirk Packaging Book, 2005.

Catherine Ryan Hyde, *Pay It Forward,* New York: Pocket, 2000.

Walter Isaacson, *Benjamin Franklin,* New York: Simon and Schuster, 2003.

Phil Jackson, Hugh Delehanty, *Sacred Hoops: Spiritual Lessons of a Hardwood Warrior,* New York: Hyperion, 1995.

David Keirsey, Marilyn Bates, *Please Understand Me,* Del Mar, CA: Prometheus Nemesis Book Company, 1984, Fourth Edition.

Pamela Walker Laird, *Pull: Networking Success Since Benjamin Franklin,* Cambridge, MA: Harvard University Press, 2006.

Robert S. Littell, *The Heart and Art of Net Weaving,* Atlanta, GA: Net Weaving International Press, 2003.

Suzanne W. Morse, *Smart Communities,* San Fransisco, CA: Jossey-Bass A Wiley Imprint, 2004.

Isabel Briggs Myers, Peter B. Myers, *Gifts Differing: Understanding Personality Type,* Mountain View, CA: Davies-Black Publishing, a division of CPP, Inc., 1995.

Robert D. Putnam, *Bowling Alone,* New York: Simon and Schuster, Inc., 2000.

Robert D. Putnam, Lewis M. Feldstein, *Better Together,* New York: Simon and Schuster, 2003.

Douglas B. Richardson, *Networking,* New York: John Wiley and Sons, 1994.

Everett M. Rogers, *Diffusion of Innovations,* New York: Free Press, A Division of Simon and Schuster, Inc., 5th Edition, 2003.

Emanuel Rosen, *The Anatomy of Buzz,* New York: Currency, published by Doubleday, 2000.

Tim Sanders, *Love is the Killer App,* New York: Three Rivers Press, 2002.

Tim Sanders, *The Likeability Factor,* New York: Crown Publishers, 2005.

Dov Seidman, *How,* Hoboken, NJ: John Wiley and Sons, 2007.

Martin E. P. Seligman, Ph.D., *What You Can Change and What You Can't,* New York: Alfred A. Knoff, 1993.

Martin E. P. Seligman, Ph.D., with Karen Reivich, MA, Lisa Jaycox, Ph.D., and Jane Gilham, Ph.D., *The Optimistic Child,* New York: Harper Collins, 1995.

Martin E. P. Seligman, Ph.D., *Authentic Happiness,* New York: The Free Press, A Division of Simon and Schuster, 2002.

Steven J. Stein, Ph.D., *The EQ Edge,* New York: Stoddart Publishing Co. Limited, 2000.

Karen Stephenson, "The Quantum Theory of Trust," UK : Financial Times, Pearson, 2006.

Compiled by Dan Zadra, *The Heart of a Volunteer,* Lynwood, WA: Compendium, Inc., 2005.

Compiled by Dan Zadra, *Be The Difference,* Seattle, WA: Compendium, Inc., 2007.

Rosamund Stone Zander, Benjamin Zander, *The Art of Possibility,* New York: Simon and Schuster, 2003.

About the Author

The author's interest in Connectors can be traced back to her father, a hub of connection in their native St. Paul. As a child, she would snuggle up with him to watch their favorite movie, *It's a Wonderful Life*. Jimmy Stewart's character—George Bailey—is given the gift of seeing what the world would have lost if he had never been born. Imprinted with this generous way of helping others build community behind the scenes, she developed the skill of being attuned to the needs of those around her and bringing others together for the common good. In her 15 years of teaching leadership to Philadelphia's executives, she has come to believe that Connectors demonstrate the kind of leadership needed in today's world.

As CEO of LEADERSHIP Philadelphia, Liz Dow is an agent of change. Once called "Philadelphia's #1 Connector" by Malcolm Gladwell, she works behind the scenes to help high-achieving professionals improve their performance, strengthen their sense of purpose, and serve the community. Prior to taking over LEADERSHIP, Liz served as a Senior Vice President with FirstUSA (now JPMorgan). She earned her MBA from the Wharton School and an MA from Cornell University. She was chosen to be a Wharton Public Policy Fellow at the White House. She has served on the boards of MEDecision, Widener University, the Philadelphia Zoo, the Please Touch Museum, Christ Church Preservation Trust, the Atwater Kent Museum of Philadelphia, the Eisenhower Exchange Fellows Selection Committee, and the regional advisory board of the Knight Foundation, and has won numerous civic awards for harnessing the power of the private sector to the public good. She was named one of the 75 Greatest Living Philadelphians in honor of the Philadelphia Eagles' 75th Anniversary.

A LEADERSHIP Fellow, class of 1986, and single parent, she has passed her passion for service on to her children. Her daughter, Scottie McQuilkin, was president of the senior class at Cornell University the same year that her son, Geoffrey Dow McQuilkin, was president of the senior class at Episcopal Academy.